HOW TO RAISE A PUPPY
YOU CAN LIVE WITH

By Clarice Rutherford and David H. Neil, M.R.C.V.S.

with illustrations by Julie Sorbie Roche,
photographs by Jan Owen

1981
Alpine Publications
Loveland, Colorado

ISBN No. 0-931866-09-X

Printed in the United States of America.

9th Printing

Cover design: Diane Burkhardt
Cover photo: Betty Jo McKinney

TO ALL THE PUPPY PEOPLE
WHO HAVE MADE A CHOICE
A Contract

I have chosen to share my life with you, a member of another species. I pledge to appreciate your uniqueness as a member of the canine family and to attempt to raise you and discipline you in terms of this uniqueness. In return, I know that you will do your best to fit into my lifestyle if it is caninely possible and will reciprocate my attentions to you by letting me share your view of the universe. I will be a better person for having this experience. I hope your life will also be better for having been with me.

CONTENTS

INTRODUCTION

"If the status quo prevails, dog ownership is going to get tougher, and deservedly so . . . The way we play it may have very significant impact on the future of the domestic dog in urban society."

The dog is our oldest domestic animal. Bones of the domestic dog were found in the Pelagawa cave region in northwestern Iraq with a radiocarbon date of 12,000 years ago. Recently, remains of the domestic dog about 14,000 years old were found in Israel. Dogs as large as wolves and as small as fox terriers lived in the ancient city of Jericho.

When one looks at the wide variety of strains of the domestic dog today one cannot help but be impressed with man's ingenuity and patience in carefully selecting and breeding dogs for different utilitarian and vital roles in his survival. The modern domestic dog reveals man's hand as he influenced the evolution of the wolf to his advantage throughout history.

However, the modern dog is in trouble. The dog problem in our cities continues and will do so until the majority of us become more aware and more responsible. Of course, there is a final solution. We can ban dogs from our cities and townships. We can even exterminate the dog! A number of cities are moving—perhaps not entirely unwittingly—toward that day. It is one solution, and it was effected in Reykjavik, Iceland. But hold on a minute. Isn't the dog worth keeping around? We think so.

Pet dogs in contemporary society have proved valuable in providing a focus of attention and love for the aged and mentally disturbed. People who live alone and are unable to get around often receive unstinting friendship from their companion dogs.

Children relate well to the family dog. During their growing years, they can share a dog's life from puppyhood to senility, feeling in the end the loss associated with the death of a dear friend. Furthermore, in an urban environment, this may be the only real contact the developing child has with an animal other than fellow human beings. The child thereby learns that animals other than man live complex lives, also experiencing joy, frustration, pain, accomplishment.

If the status quo prevails, dog ownership is going to get tougher, and deservedly so. Fellow dog owners and potential dog owners, the ball is in our court. The way we play it may have very significant impact on the future of the domestic dog in urban society.

Dog breeders, show judges, fanciers with hopes and aspirations, trialists, moms, dads, kids, unite! Share your knowledge, expertise, needs and cares. Let us together demonstrate to the disgruntled dog doubters that this wonderful and ancient relationship can be a great asset in contemporary society and that we can learn to deal with it to the mutual satisfaction of man and his dog.

We believe the most important step toward better dog-people relations begins with the way we treat a puppy from the first day we bring him home. Our main concern is in getting a puppy to respond to his master as young as possible. We believe that puppies can be taught good behavior but not by the push-pull-slap method. We believe in the effectiveness of contingent reward which includes the use of tidbits. Reward the pup with praise when he responds the way you want him to. Ignore or distract his behavior when it's not what you want, and use the scruff shake rather than the slap for discipline. Your efforts will pay off in a puppy you, and society, can live with.

We acknowledge with great appreciation the tremendous amount of knowledge of dog behavior that has been contributed by John Paul Scott, John L. Fuller and Michael W. Fox. We have benefited greatly from the books of Clarence J. Pfaffenberger, Leon F. Whitney, William E. Campbell, Daniel F. Tortora and Ian Dunbar. We have added our own observations and thoughts on puppy behavior and training with the hopes that much of the knowledge of puppy behavior can be applied by you in your home with your pup, to the benefit of man, and dog, and the quality of life in the late 20th century.

CHAPTER 1
CHOOSING YOUR PUPPY

"Do not yield to the temptation of considering only the kind of dog you loved as a kid. A big Saint Bernard, for example, might not fit your life in the city at all."

Deciding which is the best puppy for you begins before the puppy is born because behavior is first of all a hereditary factor. The personalities of the sire and dam of the puppy are an indication of the personality the pup will have, and the breed of the puppy is an important indication as to what the pup's adult behavior will be like.

When you're looking at a litter of little puppies who are so easy to handle and to control, it's much too easy to overlook the idea that within a few months this puppy will have the size and behavior characteristics of his parents and his breed, and unfortunately, you might be unhappy with the result because the little puppy has changed into a much larger and more vigorous dog than your home and lifestyle can manage. It's not the pup's fault that you didn't carefully give some thought to the adult dog that the pup would grow into. Before you even go to look at puppies, give a lot of thought to your home facilities, your lifestyle, your personality and the size and personality of dog that would best fit these. A person who would be very·content with the relatively slow-moving Bassett would be miserable with an exuberant, strong-willed Airedale. Daniel Tortora's book, *The Right Dog for You,* can be a good help in initially selecting the type of dog that is best for you.

A puppy's adult personality will be a combination of three factors, his breed, his individual genetic behavior and the socialization he received between the age of five and twelve weeks. Breed characteristics are generalizations, of course, but they are recognizable in most members of each particular breed. It's obvious to the observant person that different breeds not only look different but behave differently. For example, Huskies and Malemutes are very leader-oriented. They need to know at all times that you're the leader or they'll quickly start doing things their way. Terriers are born convinced of their own importance. Large sheepdogs need much outside activity or they can become irritable. Scent hounds are quite independent and are led by their noses, while sight hounds tend to be aloof and easily distracted by distant movements to the extent of running off. Both types of hounds do not generally display their affection by trying to please their owners. The guard dogs such as Rottweilers, Pinschers and German Shepherds need a firm attitude but when given sensible, consistent training are very loyal and dependable. Sporting breeds are often easily excited by numerous sights, sounds and smells. The miniature breeds are bright and very clever but they are also very sensitive and can easily be upset by roughness or a harsh voice. And remember, *all* breeds, large, medium and small, need exercise which can be lots of fun if you teach them running and retrieving games. However, they should not be turned loose and allowed to run the neighborhood. That kind of exercise they *don't* need. It's dangerous for the dog and inconsiderate to the neighbors.

You should be sure before acquiring a puppy that the breed characteristics will be acceptable to you and your family, your accommodations and your lifestyle. If you are an easy-going person you will not be happy at all with a leader-oriented dog who will likely become aggressive and create more problems than you can handle. A good source of information about the breed you are interested in is your local kennel club, which can give you the names of breeders. When buying a puppy you're not just buying a pedigree; you're buying the expertise and the understanding of the puppy's needs and the advice the breeder can give you based on experience with that particular breed. Another good source of information would be to attend a dog show and buy a catalog of the dogs entered. This lists the names and addresses of the people who are showing and you can follow up by contacting a breeder in your area. If this is not a possible means of contact, *Dog World* magazine is available at many newsstands listing a large number of breeders nationwide to contact. The American Kennel Club will supply names of local breeders or will give an address for the national breed club. Write to the American Kennel Club, 51 Madison Avenue, New York, NY 10010.

Read as much as you can about the history of the breed and the behavior traits and talk with other owners if possible before you finally decide which breed to select. Then buy wisely from breed experts who have a reputation to maintain. We cannot recommend buying puppies who are born in puppy mills (usually sold in pet stores). The buyer cannot learn anything about the parents of the puppy and knows nothing about the treatment the puppy received during the sensitive stages of birth to eight weeks.

When you have selected the breed that has a size and disposition best for you, it is time to consider the individual personality you want your pup to have. A good indication of this is the personality of the parent dogs. Behavior is an hereditary factor just as are the appearance, length of coat, or type of head. Therefore, if either parent is very shy or very aggressive, you may want to look at other litters before making a choice. Conversely, if the

It's important to select a puppy who has been well-socialized.

parent dogs like people and are pleasant to be around, you will know that there is a good chance the pups will have the same qualities. Chapter 5 discusses the personality traits that can be determined by using "puppy tests." Most breeders are very willing to discuss the breed and individual characteristics of their line of dogs, because the most important part of selling puppies is to see that they go to the most suitable home. The puppy will not be a carbon copy of either parent but will very likely have some of the behavior characteristics of each.

The third aspect of a puppy's personality is the socializing the pup received from the breeder and the behavior-molding the pup receives from his new master. Every breeder knows that careful breeding is only part of the story, even though a very important part. Breeders have seen a very promising puppy ruined by bad training or simply a lack of training. This is often because the new owner doesn't know about the puppy's basic needs and isn't aware of how much the puppy is capable of learning—both desirable and undesirable behaviors.

THE BEST AGE TO ACQUIRE A PUPPY

Six to eight weeks of age is generally considered the ideal age range for a puppy to leave his littermates and go to his new home. However, there are times when an older pup might seem to be a better selection for a new home. Much depends on the new owner's lifestyle and how he or she feels about starting with a very young puppy. The main concern for the new owner is to be certain that the pup has received sufficient individual attention and puppy training from the breeder since the age of six weeks.

A word of warning here: A puppy can be well socialized during the five-to-eight-week period but if he is then put in a kennel and ignored, the effect of the socialization will be diminished and the pup will again begin to show fear of strange humans or of a new environment. This is a well-known problem referred to as the "kennel-shy" syndrome. Isolation *always* has a negative effect on a dog.

Most professional breeders are conscientious about maintaining their puppies' socialization. It means a lot of work for the breeder, but a pup can be trained and introduced to various environments so that he will make a good adjustment to a new home at a later age.

There are, unfortunately, some individuals who raise puppies only for what financial gain they might get and who care nothing about the needs of the puppies. Don't hesitate to ask for specific information. Get a specific report of what care and activities have been done with the puppies, and find out how knowledgeable the person is about the characteristics and history of the breed. If the breeder seems lacking in any of these areas, don't fall victim to a hard sell. These people should not be encouraged to perpetuate their puppy activities. They do much more harm than good for the dog world.

There are many conscientious and reliable breeders who breed and raise puppies with great care. Take the time to find the right one. If the new owner wants to be certain that the older pup has been adequately socialized, he or she should arrange to take the dog for three or four days on a trial basis. If the puppy acts shy or non-responsive, the chances are strong that he is kennel or genetically shy and this is very difficult to overcome.

We have the advantage of raising and training dogs in a time when much has been discovered about the basic developmental periods of a puppy's life. This is very exciting. We can take what heredity gives us and then control the environment to develop the best possible personality in the adult dog.

CHAPTER 2
BEHAVIOR—THE ENVIRONMENTAL FACTOR

Urban living does not come naturally to a dog, but by understanding a puppy's needs, we can help him to adjust.

A major portion of this book pertains to the first six months of a puppy's life with emphasis on the first three months. There's a good reason for this. We believe that these early months are absolutely the key to molding a dog's behavior so that he can fit into the complexities of life in the 20th century. Let's face it, urban life isn't exactly a natural environment for man's best friend—but with care it can be one to which he can adapt.

Life was great for the dog in small-town America where the family dog went everywhere with the kids and also had his own circle of friends among the other dogs in the neighborhood. In contrast, most dogs today live isolated lives in backyards, pens or homes, competely at the mercy of a few members of the family

who often are very busy with other activities. If the dog is fed every day and has shelter, we are too likely to think that we're filling his needs.

The dog is by nature a pack animal with definite social needs. Through the centuries while man and dog were evolving, the dog developed empathy with humans and a desire for attention from his human pack members. If this need for attention is ignored the dog can become very frustrated and might well begin to indulge in activities like incessant barking and destroying property. If the dog is not only kept in such an environment as an adult, but is bred and raised with inadequate attention, the problem is compounded.

Dog behavior studies have determined that the first twelve weeks of a dog's life are vitally important because a puppy's experiences during this time will affect his emotional responses as an adult dog. It stands to reason, then, that if we know how the puppy is growing and what the puppy needs during these different stages, we can help every puppy get the best possible start in life.

The need for human attention begins shortly after the puppy is born. During the first few weeks of life the pup is going through the most amazing process of growth. At first, his world is dark and silent and consists solely of contact with his littermates and the constant care of his mother. After about two weeks he begins to learn new behaviors which will adapt him well to living in a sensory and social world. By eight weeks of age he has full use of his sensory and motor systems and his central nervous system has reached maturity, ready for whatever learning experiences await.

The puppy's central nervous system, and therefore his behavior, develops in a wondrously particular and precise pattern, and each stage of growth has an effect on the puppy's actions. If the pup doesn't have his physical and social needs satisfied during any one of these periods, certain characteristics of his personality will be stalled at that particular stage of development. This in turn will have an effect on how the dog will behave when he is older.

For example, some dogs remain overly suspicious of anything new or different, often because they never developed investigative behavior when it was a normal part of their growing up (eight to twelve weeks). Another dog might be too easily excited, to the extent of appearing hyperactive, as a result of not having had adequate environmental stimulation during the stage of learning how to sort out sounds, sights and smells (six to ten weeks). And both the shy and the hyperactive personality can be strongly affected by a lack of human contact from three to seven weeks.

You are undoubtedly wondering if knowing about these developmental stages in a puppy's life is all that important. Obviously, many dog owners have raised very fine dogs without such information—for good reasons. These pups may have had outgoing personalities and have been able to overcome some lack of socialization. Even more likely, these pups were fortunate enough to be raised in homes where their needs were automatically and unknowingly met during each period. Dogs have been successfully socialized for over 10,000 years without anyone being specifically aware of it, let alone labeling the process!

So it is today in many homes. Puppies who get a lot of attention and receive touch, sound and visual stimulation in the course of a normal day grow up to be healthy, well-adjusted dogs.

But not all puppies are so carefully raised. If the breeder is away from home during the day, for instance, a certain amount of time must be reserved in the evening for puppy activities. This is why timing the arrival of a litter is important. A concerned breeder checks the calendar when planning a breeding to make sure that puppies will not be neglected. If certain social obligations or an unusually heavy work load will occur at a certain time of the year, a litter should not be bred to arrive at such a time.

The breeder who is not willing to give some time to the puppies should let someone else do the breeding and puppy raising. There are enough "weirdo" dogs in the world now that did not get the people-care they needed while they were puppies.

This is where the so-called "puppy mills" are totally negligent. The people who operate these mills have a large number of female dogs whose only function is to produce puppies for profit and who are often kept isolated in cages, boxes, or other very small areas. This so-called "breeder" has no understanding of the needs of the dog and does not realize the damage done to a pup's personality by giving it no socialization during the first eight weeks. It is not only extreme cruelty to keep the parent dogs in such confining isolation, but it is also cruel to the puppies to deny them the socialization they must have if they are to adjust to living with people as they grow up.

Today, so much has been learned about dog behavior that there is no excuse for a socially maladjusted dog. Whether you are a breeder who is introducing the world of dogs to newcomers, or whether you are a first-time puppy owner, there is much you can do to make this a good world for your pet. You don't have the luxury of many days and weeks to be a partner in your puppy's personality development. But you don't have to give up a normal routine and become a "puppy-recluse" in order to accomplish your goal. Mostly, you just need to be aware of what's going on in the natural process as a newborn puppy grows from a blob into a bouncing young adult.

CHAPTER 3
THE DEVELOPMENTAL PERIOD
(The First Three Months)

Experiences during the first three months are the foundation of the puppy's mature personality.

The first three months of a dog's life are called the developmental months because it is during this time that almost all of the dog's basic behavior patterns are developed. The first seven weeks of the puppy's life are the responsibility of the breeder. Beyond that age, the responsibility for socialization shifts to the new owner. Each period has specific activities that can help a puppy grow emotionally.

There are three basic developmental periods in the first twelve weeks. These periods are defined here by calendar time, but this doesn't mean that all puppies will begin each period on exactly the same day. There will be variances depending upon the breed and on individual differences within the litter. Littermates usually catch up with each other, however, by the end of the last period.

Table 1. Basic Developmental Periods

Neonatal Period	Transitional Period	Socialization
1-14 days	15-21 days	22-84 days
birth to 2 weeks	2 to 3 weeks	3-12 weeks

In order for us to understand a puppy's needs as he begins to grow, we should become familiar with the characteristics of the different periods. This chapter will cover the general description of each period. Chapter 4 will discuss the breeder's role in raising puppies, and Chapters 6 and 7 will deal with the new owner's activities in taking a puppy to his new home.

THE NEONATAL PERIOD

1-14 days	**Key Puppy Behavior:** Spends about 90 percent of time sleeping Susceptible to excess heat or cold Crawls Nurses Seeks warmth of littermates and mother Can usually right himself if turned over Needs anal stimulation for urination and defecation

At this stage the bitch is the main influence on the puppy. Her health, milk supply, and attitude toward the pups, and later toward people who come to look at the puppies, will influence the behavioral development of the litter. If she is overly fearful or aggressive, this can be imprinted on the puppies and their future behavior might be very similar to hers whether or not they were born with a fearful or aggressive genetic trait. Thus a behavior can be either genetically or environmentally derived.

At this age the pup's abilities are confined to sucking, vocalizing, and crawling slowly. The senses of sight and hearing are not functional yet. The eyes may begin to open around ten days of age but in most cases are not open until about fourteen days of age.

The puppy learns about his environment through touch. You can observe him crawling around, moving his head from side to side until he bumps into his mother or a littermate. A puppy might crawl away from the bitch, but she should be able to retrieve him by carrying him in her mouth, providing he doesn't crawl out of her sight or sound. Urination and defecation are reflex responses that occur only when the bitch licks her puppies' anal and genital region.

During this period the pup is aware only of heat, cold and pain. He is not yet capable of regulating body heat efficiently and therefore needs his mother and the other puppies to help maintain his own warmth. Even though it looks as though the pups do nothing but eat and sleep, this is a very important period. The central nervous system is rapidly developing, getting ready for the next stage.

THE TRANSITIONAL PERIOD

15-21 days	**Key Puppy Behavior:**
	Eyes open
	Teeth begin to emerge
	Gets up on four legs and takes a few steps
	Begins to lap liquids
	Defecates without the mother's stimulation

The puppy's eyesight is dim, but he is ready for the next adventure. He discovers that the other pups are more than just warm lumps to be crawled over and slept on. He begins to stagger around on four legs, lifting himself up first on his front legs, then on the hind legs as they become equally strong. Activity periods are brief, followed by sleep to gather strength for the next concentrated effort. By the end of this transitional period, the pup can walk on four legs and lap milk or soft food in a fairly efficient manner (although not very elegantly).

The pup no longer needs constant care from the bitch and is beginning to defecate without her stimulus. He starts to get interested in littermates. The very beginnings of pack-oriented behavior, such as pawing at each others' faces and chewing on littermates' ears, are seen at this stage.

THE SOCIALIZATION PERIOD

Socialization is the name given to the next nine weeks, the growth period lasting from three to twelve weeks of age. We have found that this period can be divided into four stages, each of which is an important stepping-stone for the one that follows.

The dog's primary social relationships develop during this time. If his primary relationships are with people, the pup will be able to form lasting relationships throughout his life, but the puppy who receives little human contact during this time will find it difficult to adjust to humans as long as he lives.

The puppy also needs to be with littermates and the bitch during the first weeks of the socialization period. He needs to learn how to act around other members of his own species, or he could become a dog that picks fights easily or has problems with mating (if this should subsequently be desired).

The Period of Becoming Aware
(First Stage of Socialization)

22-28 days	Key Puppy Behavior:
3-4 weeks	Can hear
	Begins to eat food
	Begins to bark, wag tail, and bite other pups
4-5 weeks	Uses legs quite well but tires easily
	Paws
	Bares teeth
	Growls
	Chases
	Plays prey-killing games

We have divided the socialization period into four stages not only for ease of discussion but also because the behavior patterns of the puppy are readily distinguishable and determined by their physical age. The central nervous system continues to develop rapidly during this time. The puppy now has both sight and hearing ability and by four weeks is beginning to develop perception of distance.

The beginning of the socialization period can be determined for each puppy by using the startle-reaction test. *When a puppy visibly reacts to a loud sound, he is into the socialization stage.* This is also a means of telling which pups are on a slightly different time schedule in their physical development. This is valuable information because otherwise these pups might unjustly be labeled as dull-witted or slow when actually the only problem is that they need time to catch up physically with the others. Puppies, however, don't always go by the book and react on the twenty-first or twenty-second day. One breeder accidentally dropped a pan about four feet from the puppies on the eighteenth day and got a big reaction. On the twenty-first day the puppies didn't react to a loud noise. By then they apparently accepted it as part of their world.

Even if we didn't look at the calendar or use the startle test, we would know when this period begins. It's as if someone pushed the "on" button. Virtually overnight, the puppy turns into an animated little being.

From twenty-two to twenty-eight days, the puppy is experiencing a shower of sensory stimulation. So much awareness of the world around him is happening so suddenly that the pup needs a very stable home environment to balance the excess stimulation. The bitch should remain with the litter as much as possible during this week.

By the end of the third week, the pup displays much more complex behavior than at the beginning of the period, which is an indication of how rapidly development occurs. The pups now play together. They start to learn how much chewing and biting the other pups will take. They begin to show adult behavior patterns with their play-fighting, scruff-holding and prey-killing (head shaking) movements and they are beginning to bark, growl and snap at each other. Some pups begin barking and wagging tails around three weeks of age, but this varies with the breed and the individuals.

It is possible for many of a puppy's behavior patterns to get stalled at this stage because he isn't allowed to act normally during the next two periods. This occurs especially among the toy breeds because of attitudes toward their size, but it can happen with any breed. When a puppy is not ever allowed to act like a dog (i.e., rough and tumble playing with other pups, investigating all corners of his world), never experiences stress of any kind, and has all his needs met before they even arise, he becomes a spoiled pet, a perpetual puppy. The breeder is cheating the dog by not allowing him to develop into a mature canid and the owner is cheating himself of the pleasure of having a mature dog as a companion.

The Period of Curiosity
(Second Stage of Socialization)

36-49 days	**Key Puppy Behavior:**
5-7 weeks	Weaning begins
	Curious
	Little sense of fear
	Participates in group activities and sexual play
	Dominance order is beginning

This is an *extremely important* time in the puppy's life. It is the period when the pup is totally dependent on the environment you provide for him to stimulate and develop his genetic qualities. In addition to needing a stimulating environment the pup must receive attention from people. The kinds of experiences a puppy has during this period have a very strong effect on how he will react emotionally to humans when he is an adult. If he has little contact with people, except for being fed, he's probably not going to find it easy to accept human attention when he's older.

This is another time of rapid growth and change. During this period a puppy acquires full use of his eyes and ears, his legs become stronger and more coordinated, and his brain reaches a final stage of physical development. Further development now largely depends on the experiences encountered by the otherwise fully-equipped puppy.

At the beginning of this period, the puppy still has little sense of fear and is quick to approach anything and anybody. But by the end of these two weeks he begins to be more cautious in his approach, which is all a part of learning to discriminate among sights, sounds and smells. Pups who don't go through these two periods of learning (having been isolated or overprotected) tend to become hyperactive adults. They have not learned how to sort out sights, sounds and smells during these weeks and to identify the significant ones.

Sexual play is evident at this age. Mounting is quite common among male puppies and sometimes females mount other puppies also. This is a normal part of puppy play and is important in teaching puppies what is normal sexual response as they mature. While mature males tend generally to confine their mounting to females, mounting to signify dominance over another male continues in maturity. Females also sometimes mount other females as a demonstration of dominance.

Many behaviorists agree that socialization reaches a peak by the forty-ninth day. From here on, human relationships, though still very important, begin to have a decreasing effect on the socialization of the puppy. In other words, the amount of individual attention a puppy has received by the forty-ninth day can never be made up without a proportionately larger expenditure of time and effort.

The seventh week (forth-ninth day) is considered by many breeders to be the right age for a puppy to go to his new home. By then the pup has had sufficient time with his littermates for developing adequate dog behavior patterns. His new owner can easily become the pack leader and can give the pup individual attention and a lot of environmental variety.

The Period of Behavioral Refinement
(Third Stage of Socialization)

50-63 days	Key Puppy Behavior
7-9 weeks	7 weeks: Has total hearing and visual capacity Will investigate anything 8 weeks: Fearful of sudden and loud sounds and movement Cautious of anything new in the environment

The period of behavioral refinement is characterized by progression from unfettered curiosity to a more nervous evaluation of the stimulus created by the pup's environment. This reaches its height around eight weeks of age and persists to about ten weeks of age.

This stage is an important milestone in a puppy's life. He reaches full visual and hearing capacity, and his brain is physically mature. This means the brain is ready to perform its physical processes and the pup can start learning to respond to your wishes as long as the learning process is taking place in very small steps. However, this doesn't mean he's ready to be treated as an adult dog. He is still emotionally very immature.

This age is sometimes termed the "fear period" because the pup is very susceptible to long-lasting effects if he receives a bad fright during this time. Dr. Michael Fox has observed that at five and six weeks a puppy can be severely frightened and in a relatively short period of time bounce back to his normal happy self again. However, during the eighth week, if the pup receives a bad fright, it may take weeks for him to return to his normal behavior in the same frightening situation. He may even carry the fear all his life. A loud, rough person, a spanking, or an abnormally sharp noise are examples of frights that can cause such a reaction. Thus, shipping a puppy to a new home by air freight during the eighth week could have a lasting bad effect. But don't think you have to go to the other extreme and be overly protective, keeping your pup in seclusion. Let him have normal experiences.

Puppies at this age also become hesitant about new and different objects and situations. During the preceding period (five to seven weeks) the puppy usually approached the unfamiliar fearlessly. Now, at eight weeks, the pup is noticeably more hesitant in his approach. He may go back again and again to the same area or object as though he doesn't trust his initial judgment.

An example of this caution is seen with retrievers—the five-to seven-week old puppy will splash in shallow water or happily bounce into heavy grass, cattails, or whatever is in his path. But during his eighth week this same pup will start to be suspicious of water, even a shallow pond, or a pile of rocks, and he seems to think that diving into a patch of weeds is unthinkable, at least without a lot of sniffing and investigating first. However, by the end of the ninth week this very pup is returning to his previous crash-bang self.

A house puppy is cautious, too. Watch how he reacts to a new piece of furniture being brought into his room.

This is all another normal and important part of the socializing process, a continuation of sorting out the multitude of smells, sounds and sights to determine what is important.

The Period of Environmental Awareness
(Fourth Stage of Socialization)

64-84 days	**Key Puppy Behavior:**
9-12 weeks	Develops strong dominant and subordinate behavior among littermates
	Begins to learn right behavior for right time
	Continues to improve in motor skills
	Has very short attention span

Even though no new behavior patterns are evident during these weeks, the pup is beginning to learn the right behaviors for the right times. This is no small task, and it is a necessary stage for the pup to go through in the maturing process. His brain is ready for full functioning, but information must be fed into it one step at a time. It takes a puppy a long time to learn the acceptable ways of the world. This age is the culmination of the socialization process. Exposure to different environments (as discussed in Chapter 6) is the primary consideration here.

Up to this age the puppy has been very self-oriented. Most of his learning has been "me"-directed. He has learned to like his new family. He knows where his bed is, where the food is kept, where there's a warm place for a nap, and (very importantly) where the urinating and defecating areas are. Now he's beginning to pay attention to *you*.

In fact, he thinks you're wonderful! He'll quickly learn his name. He'll come flying to you when you call him and get his attention. At this age, the puppy has a strong desire to please. After all, you're his whole world, having taken the place of mother and littermates.

The puppy pays attention to you, but he's also extremely busy learning everything he can about the world around him. The pup's brain tissue reached its full physiological growth around eight weeks of age and now he's ready to learn, to have experiences that will teach him how to behave, how to act like a dog, how to please a human—quite a challenge for a pup, but one that he's ready for.

By ten weeks of age, strong dominant and subordinate behavior is displayed among littermates and has been evident for three to four weeks in some cases. Any littermates remaining together should be kept in separate housing by ten weeks of age. Some puppies seem to get along together better than others, but they should still be separated except for occasional short exercise periods. Otherwise, one puppy will probably develop a more dominant personality and another a more subordinate personality than they would have if separated. In addition, the puppies will be so involved with each other that they will lose their interest in people and will become much more difficult to train.

The last stage of socialization is a most delightful one. At the same time that you should be actively molding your puppy's behavior (he won't always be this small and eager to please) you should also be enjoying your puppy. Relax and have fun. A puppy stays little such a short time—he'll be grown up before you know it.

Developmental Periods of the First Three Months.

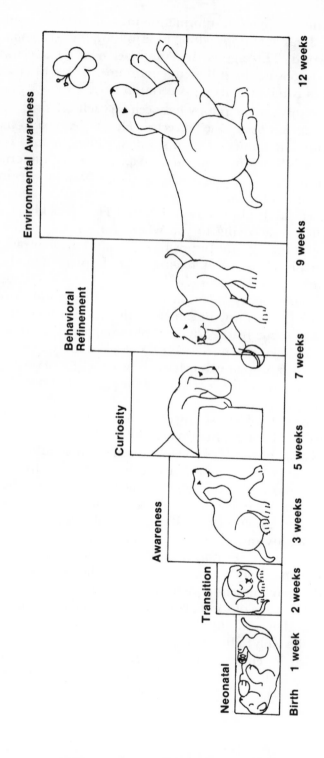

| Birth | 1 week | 2 weeks | 3 weeks | 5 weeks | 7 weeks | 9 weeks | 12 weeks |

Neonatal

Transition

Awareness

Curiosity

Behavioral Refinement

Environmental Awareness

Table 3. Summary of Puppy Behavior—What You Can Expect

Age	Behavior
1 and 2 weeks	All activities are innate—only sucking, crying, crawling and touching. No sense of sight or sound. Is susceptible to cold temperatures. Must receive touching from bitch to stimulate elimination. Cannot learn anything at this age.
3 weeks	Eyesight and hearing dim but rapidly improving. Begins to walk briefly. Becomes interested in littermates. Able to start eating and drinking and to eliminate without the bitch's stimulus.
4 weeks	Needs a very stable environment. Becomes aware of multitude of sights and sounds. Learns that people are important. Should remain with bitch as much as possible.
5 weeks	Life becomes exciting! Not afraid of anything. Is very aware of people and likes to be with them.
6 weeks	Has full use of eyes and ears. Legs stronger and more coordinated. Investigates everything in sight.
7 weeks	Very involved with his own needs. Will seldom respond to name. (You must take initiative if you want him to follow you.) Can be started on housebreaking routine.
8 weeks	Occasionally responds to name. Hesitant about approaching new things. Needs to be able to take his own time about new experiences.
9 weeks	Will follow at your side for short distances. Likes to lie down beside or on top of your feet.
10–12 weeks	Almost always responds to name and comes when called from short distance. Will come running when he hears food pan rattle. Learns not to get stepped on. Becomes more dependable with housebreaking.

CHAPTER 4
THE BREEDER'S RESPONSIBILITY
(The First Seven Weeks)

A puppy's most important behavioral needs during his first seven weeks are:
- **a stimulating environment**
- **exposure to mild stress**
- **individual attention**

Whether a litter is raised in the house or out in the kennel, whether the breed is a house dog or a sporting dog, there's much a breeder can do to encourage the development of emotionally healthy puppies.

Being a breeder of puppies is a very important job, one that should be undertaken with the commitment of the time and effort necessary to get the pups off to the best possible start.

Aside from a clean, warm home box area and adequate food, a young puppy has definite behavioral needs. During the first seven weeks, a puppy's three most important needs are a stimulating environment, exposure to mild stress, and individual attention. These needs can readily be met by the breeder if he or she recognizes them and then adjusts time schedules and the home environment to best satisfy the emotional growth requirements of the puppies.

ENVIRONMENTAL ENRICHMENT

The first two weeks of a puppy's life are in a separate world from the rest of his life. Even the instinctive behaviors that a puppy exhibits at this age aren't carried over into the "dog-behavior" world. Therefore, the breeder can't provide much enrichment during the first two weeks because the pup lives in his own silent, dark world. Environmental enrichment at this age consists of seeing that the mother is healthy and well fed and that the litter is in a warm, comfortable, clean area. During the puppy's third week, he's very engrossed in the mini-world of littermates and puppy-box area and consequently is not very receptive to environmental stimulations.

However, beginning with the fourth week (around twenty-two days of age), and from then on until seven weeks of age, the puppy is very busy learning to use his rapidly developing senses. You might ask if providing environmental stimulation is worth the bother for such a short period of time, from twenty-one to forty-nine days. Yes, it certainly is. We know from behavioral and physiological studies how rapidly the pup's nervous system is growing during these weeks. The breeder and the puppy's new master probably receive the greatest future rewards for the relatively small effort put forth during these days.

Something as common as a lawn chair can provide environmental enrichment.

Three through Seven Weeks

You don't need to dazzle the puppy with a clutter of items. Over-stimulation certainly isn't the goal. Do your pups play in the backyard? The lawn furniture is an example of environmental stimulation. Moving the wheelbarrow around for cleanup is another example. This is what we mean when we say that a litter raised in a family home environment is automatically socialized and stimulated. However, when puppies are raised in a more isolated area of a pen or kennel, specific items need to be added to their environment.

Spending a lot of money isn't necessary. Use whatever is available to you. For example, set a couple of old wood stumps in the pen area. Cardboard boxes are marvelous and fall in the easy-come, easy-go category. These can be dens for a pup to go into or tunnels to walk through. One item that's very popular with one breeder's pups is a wood box about four feet long and two feet wide. It has two openings on diagonal ends of the long sides with carpet on the floor. The pup can go in one door and out the other or lie inside and look out, or run through, or whatever seems right at the time. Another good idea is short lengths of plastic or ceramic pipe—whichever size your pups can easily walk through. (Never take a chance with a pipe that might become too narrow as the puppies grow.)

One item we consider almost essential for puppies is a platform of at least two steps, not too high for your five- to six-week old puppy to navigate easily. The steps should have a large enough area on top so that the pup can feel comfortable before starting down again.

Use your imagination. Look around at garage sales and see what you can find. Safety is the primary concern. Sharp edges or material that can be easily shredded and possibly swallowed should not be used.

By four weeks of age, the puppy starts to leave the box or home base area to defecate and urinate. It can help the pup begin to learn the significance of carpeting if the sleeping box has carpet in it or if there is a narrow strip of carpet around the box so that his feet touch on the way out but he goes past it to tend to his chores. This gives him another texture to feel, as well as giving him the idea that carpeting is only for sleeping and sitting and walking.

Puppies can begin to associate carpeting with their clean home box area which aids house-training.

Toys

Toys can add much variety to a puppy's environment. The first concern in selecting toys is safety; obviously they should not be breakable or sharp. Toys which can be left with puppies in their play area are pieces of hard wood dowling cut to lengths that extend no more than one or two inches on either side of the puppy's mouth, and pieces of hard leather. From four weeks on, puppies like to mouth things and will use some of these items in "catch me if you can" games.

A wide range of chewing and play toys is available in pet supply stores but a puppy isn't interested in how much money you do or don't spend on toys. For a young pup, the important criterion is something he can pick up in his mouth or push and roll with his nose. Four-ounce cans (tomato sauce, for example) from the grocery shelf, with both ends smoothly removed, make enjoyable toys for some puppies who love to push them with their noses and make them roll, sometimes picking them up and carrying them briefly. Small cardboard frozen-juice containers are also excellent for this type of toy.

Puppies have preferences and what attracts one may not interest another. A litter fortunate enough to live in a natural environment will probably find all the toys they need in pieces of twigs, leaves, pieces of bark and the various items of nature that are about. Winter puppies or small breeds who are in a house or small kennel area need to have toys provided for them. The size of the pups would be a factor here. A toy has no value if it's too large, and it's dangerous if too small. A sturdy glove is a good toy; for example, a worn-out leather work glove is ideal. Think of the wealth of odors it has! A couple of knotted socks of different textures can be a lot of fun.

Old stuffed toys that have been rejected by previous owners can make good toys for some pups but obviously not for the type that will immediately rip them apart. The use of this toy will depend on your breed and your particular pups. Button eyes should be taken out.

Feel free to experiment with household rejects that might make good toys for *your* pup. A puppy doesn't need a large number of toys as he grows up. A knotted sock to shake, a leather glove to carry around and a couple of pieces of hard leather to chew are probably all the wealth he'll need from the age of four weeks on.

EXPOSURE TO MILD STRESS

Even though the bitch is the primary influence in the puppy's life for the first twenty-one days, the breeder can already begin to influence a puppy's future behavior. Although the pup's eyes don't open until the end of the second week and his hearing isn't functioning until the third week, he will respond on a purely physical level to being touched. Touching and lifting the pup begin to condition his physiology to react at a very low level to changes in his experience.

Breeders who have made a practice of handling pups at a very young age have observed that these pups become very outgoing and confident as they get older. Now, fortunately, there is a study which verifies and expands this observation. Dr. Michael Fox, after conducting a study on the heart rates of puppies, concluded that mildly stressing puppies during the first five weeks will develop dogs who are superior when put in learning or competitive situations. Puppies who are handled at an early age and exposed to mild stress on a physiological level are better able to handle stress later in their lives without becoming emotionally disturbed or indulging in hyperactive behavior. As a result, they learn quickly and are more responsive to new experiences in different environments.

Exposing puppies to stress is not another word for cruelty. We are referring to a *mild* stress. For the first two weeks, it involves picking up the pups on a regular basis. Many breeders automatically do this if they weigh the puppies regularly or if they just pick up each puppy each day to admire it. Putting the pup on the scale for weighing is an acceptable type of mild stress. However, a family with young children must take care that the children don't handle the pups at this age. Too much handling would be much worse than none at all.

During the first week pick the puppy up each day. Rub his softness against your cheek, admire his miniature perfection— these are the fringe benefits. Hold him for about a minute, the puppy's body firmly supported with your hand under his tummy. Weigh him if you desire.

During the second week, seven to fourteen days, begin holding the pups in different positions briefly. On one day turn the pup in a circle to the right, the next day to the left; the next day hold him upright, then the next day in a head-down position briefly. On one day during this week put the pup in a cold room for two minutes (a refrigerator will do the job if that's the only cold alternative).

Occasionally you will find a puppy who stiffens when picked up. This pup should be given the same routine as the others. If anything, he needs the brief but gentle stimulation to a greater degree than the others. But don't overdo it. More is not better. Pick him up gently once a day and then let him alone. This little guy will probably be a shy puppy, one who hesitates about everything and everybody in his environment. He will need to be placed in a quiet home and could make a fine companion for an older person. This pup should never be used in a breeding program no matter how beautiful he may be, and he or she should be neutered or spayed.

It also happens infrequently that a pup will show signs of brain damage, such as being able to move only in a tight circle. If you observe unusual behavior, consult your veterinarian about the severity of your particular case.

During the third week, fifteen to twenty-one days, the stress can be more specific. On one day, pick up the puppy and give a momentary pinch to his ear with your thumb and forefinger. Though he may cry out he should calm very quickly. The next day, pick the puppy up and give him a momentary pinch between his front toes.

The fourth week, twenty-two to twenty-eight days, is a very stimulating one for the puppy. He is aware of all the many sights and sounds around him and is quite excitable. Because of this excitability, we feel that one stress event is sufficient for this week. About midway during the week, we like to take the pup from his littermates and put him on a different floor surface than he has experienced before. As well as being a stress activity for the puppy, this is also valuable for observation of the pup's behavior and probably doesn't take more than three to four minutes per puppy.

Put the puppy down on cement, wood, dirt or fine gravel, or linoleum if it isn't too slick for walking. If the area is bare we will place a jacket on the floor, or put in a chair or anything that represents a different object for the pup to either approach or ignore. After you have put the pup down on the floor, begin to record how he reacts to being alone, how quickly he begins to cry, whether he walks around or stays in one place, or if he's investigating with tail wagging.

We include this record of behavior in our puppy testing analysis (see page 46). In this respect, the time spent with the puppy at this age is for our own benefit. The importance from the puppy's view is the lifting and touching by a person as he is removed from his littermates and the exposure to a different floor surface which provides a minor stress to which he can adjust.

The breeder can already begin to see differences in personality in the litter and it's interesting to keep a record of these. Make a note of which pups are the most aggressive feeders and which ones lose out in competition and seem to always end up on the outside of the puppy pile. Which pups are the noisiest? Which squirm and cry when picked up and which settle down and enjoy it?

The most extreme behaviors stand out first, of course, but don't forget to notice the pups who are in the middle range of temperament. These are the pups who likely will be easily trainable as they grow older.

If you have a large litter of all the same color, a dot of fingernail polish in different areas on the puppies will help you identify them (right ear, left ear, middle of head, each shoulder, tail, etc.). You can also use a different color yarn for each puppy's neck.

During *the fifth week,* twenty-nine to thirty-five days, we give the pups mild auditory and visual stress. On one of the days play a radio near the home box area when the pups are awake. Play it at a loud but not blaring level. If you have normal hearing and it sounds loud but not irritating to you, it will be sufficient. Five minutes is enough. This can be repeated again later in the day for another five minutes.

On another day of this week, give the puppy some mild visual stress. A very large cardboard box can be rigged up for this with lights inserted at levels where the puppy can see them going on and off. Four or five flashlights, manipulated by helpers, can be a sufficient number. Have the flashlights turned on and off for two to three minutes.

By the end of the fifth week, the mild stress activities become a minor factor and the individual attention by the breeder takes over as the major aspect of the activities. Minor stress is still important and will continue to be a part of the individual attention, because there is a certain amount of stress every time the puppy is removed from his littermates and taken to a different place where he is expected to pay attention to you.

INDIVIDUAL ATTENTION

Personal attention is important because it helps the puppy to develop a feeling of his importance as an individual. This in turn helps him to grow into a happy dog who is eager to please his owner. Your time alone with your puppy also helps him learn that the name of the game is to be with people and to pay attention to people.

During the puppy's first three weeks, he isn't emotionally aware of the person who gives him individual attention because his central nervous system hasn't reached that stage of development yet. The purpose during these weeks is to acquaint the puppy physically to the human touch and with a slight level of stress. From four weeks of age on, however, the puppy will be aware of you as a person. Individual attention will help to imprint on the pup his place in the world of humans.

The fourth week is the beginning of the socialization period. There's no big mystery about socializing puppies; it consists of very simple, normal activities. It's just that the *socialization must be done.* The time is so short and goes so rapidly that often, even with the best of intentions on the part of the breeder and the new owner, pups don't get the variety of experiences they need.

Puppies this age should have continuing human contact. A few minutes of individual attention for each pup during this week is important. We like to use our time for introducing each puppy to a new floor surface (discussed in the mild stress section). At least one other time this week, each puppy can be picked up, petted and talked to.

By the *fifth week*, twenty-nine to thirty-five days, the central nervous system has developed to an amazing degree. The puppies now have both sight and sound and are beginning to develop perception of distance. However, even though the pups need the stimulation of people, sights and sounds, emotionally they are still very immature, and they tire easily, so a little attention goes a long way. At least once during this week, but preferably twice, the breeder should take each puppy away from the puppy-pen area for at least ten mintues. The time can be spent with informal play. Bend down to the pup's level as much as possible.

This is a good age for *new* people and children to play with the puppies, provided caution is taken to see that the pups aren't overstimulated. In fact, if there are no children in the home, it's a

A puppy needs personal attention to help him learn confidence in himself and in people.

good idea to invite a child to come and see the puppies. (The pups can have the needle-sharp points of their nails trimmed off.)

During the *sixth week*, thirty-six to forty-two days, it would be a catastrophy if you neglected to give each pup individual attention. It puts you in the category of being a producer, not a breeder, and you should never again have another litter in your care. (Yes, it's that important!)

The puppy's attitude toward people is noticeably changing now. When you took each puppy away from his littermates during the fourth week, the puppy was too young to be interested in any interaction with you. Even last week, the pup probably wasn't too interested in you personally, but now at this age most pups will run towards you and try to climb in your lap or jump on your legs. A two-way communication system is developing.

The process of building self-confidence and a good feeling about himself (yes, dogs need this too) begins right now, at this young age. *A total of twenty minutes spent with each puppy away from the litter this week, preferably in two ten-minute sessions, is the best thing you can do to help that puppy begin to develop a happy personality.*

Occasionally, you'll have a puppy who will be very unhappy when removed from his littermates. This pup may act shy and be quite uncomfortable when taken to a different place. He may not want to come to you or may not even want to walk around and investigate the area by himself. When working with this puppy during his individual attention session, be sure you are where the pup can neither see nor hear his littermates. Sit down on the floor or ground near the pup. Don't lean over him; that will only make him more fearful. Talk to him in a quiet voice. Pat your hand on the floor in front of him. Try to get his attention. See if you can coax him to come to you even if it's just a matter of his moving a few inches. This pup needs much gentleness. If you're an impatient person, don't try anything that will make you irritated when the pup doesn't respond the way you think he should. Just spend the time sitting close to the puppy. If neither of you moves for the first session or two, that's the way it is. The puppy will gradually become accustomed to your presence and will begin to approach you and investigate. This puppy will need to be placed in a family that is willing to work with this personality type and should be spayed or neutered. For the average rambunctious puppy, petting, playing and talking to him are easy to do.

The first session at the beginning of the seventh week, forty-three to forty-nine days (or the last session of the sixth week), should be the puppy-testing routine which ideally should be done by a stranger to the pups. The second individual session this week should be about ten mintues long with each puppy and should include the same puppy-testing activities. The remainder of the session can be spent simply walking near the puppy while he sniffs and explores and sitting down on his level for a short time with some gentle play. Talk to the pup, too. Try to get his attention with your voice.

A repetition of the puppy-testing activities is not for the purpose of recording the test again but as a good procedure for getting the pup to pay attention to you. These can be considered as excellent pre-training activities.

By the end of this week, many puppies will be going to their new homes. The breeder can be confident that he or she has given the puppies every advantage possible in preparing them for their new life in their new packs.

OTHER CONSIDERATIONS FOR THE BREEDER

Weaning

If physiology and nutrition were our only concerns, the bitch could quickly become unnecessary to the pups because of the advancements of modern science. During the first few days she has kept them warm and, because of her own vaccinations, she has given them passive immunity to infectious disease through antibodies in her colostrum milk (the first milk after parturition). Beyond this point, milk mixtures are available that can replace the bitch's milk nutritionally. Theoretically, if this is all that weaning is, the pups could now be removed from the bitch. However, we think weaning goes beyond the purely nutritional aspects and that it is a developmental process affecting the dog's future social adjustment.

The interaction of the puppies with the bitch and with littermates is profoundly important for at least the first five weeks. If you want a puppy who is well-adjusted to his identity as a canid, then his relationships with other dogs are very important. For example, the puppy learns from his littermates or his mother just how much of a bite is too much. He learns through this experience that he must control the use of his jaws.

Puppies must first associate with their own kind before they can develop affection with people.

As the pup approaches the age of five weeks, the period of curiosity, he begins to explore and will leave his mother and his littermates at times. Among wild canids, other adult members of the pack would interact with the pup, but with the domestic dog this is the point at which people begin to take over the role of the canine mother, virtually reliving history and in doing so reinforcing the domestication of the puppy into the human world. Weaning is part of that domestication.

A breeder shouldn't accept any one specific rule for the weaning of pups. Much depends on the size of the litter, the size of the pups and the attitude and health of the bitch. If the bitch's attitude and health permit, we think it best to keep her with the pups for at least four weeks. For the next one to two weeks we recommend nursing only three or four times a day and then completely taking the pups off the bitch. Supplemental feeding can begin at three weeks of age, which is often beneficial to both bitch and pups.

Raising the Single Puppy

Raising the single puppy whose mother has been able to nurse and associate with him is not very much different from raising a whole litter. You are the sole controller of socialization, however, as we presume there are no other young dogs around. The more profound effects of not having littermates will be seen later—for instance, the early sexual play that occurs around six weeks is associated not only with sexual behavior but with dominance and submission. This type of dog-to-dog interaction, of course, cannot be simulated, so there is nothing we can substitute. We believe that for this reason and perhaps also because of deprivation of interactions between three and four weeks, the lone puppy may always have an awkwardness with other dogs in adult life. But this is not absolutely certain. If you find another young dog for yours to play with at least as early as twelve weeks of age onwards, this may be adequate compensation.

The hand-reared pup who has neither mother nor littermates is a more serious matter. Dr. Michael Fox has noted that a puppy must recognize and be accepted by his own kind before he can relate well to a person. Many aspects of behavior can be learned only by interaction with the pup's own species, such as the social releasers of barking, tail-wagging, paw-raising and genital-olfactory exploration. The hand-reared pup might appear "loveless" toward humans for this reason.

If you are raising a single puppy, you must handle your puppy a number of times a day—more than normal in the early weeks-in order to avoid social deprivation, say four to six times a day for a total of at least twenty minutes. Lie down with him and allow him to bite and growl, threaten, bare his teeth, etc. You must interact like his missing littermates. Do not play roughly or violently. When puppy sinks his teeth too hard and hurts—push him away, growl and squeal, and then isolate him for several minutes. This way he learns the social limits of play, useful subsequently with other dogs and people. If you must punish, do it like the bitch—hold the scruff of the neck and shake a few times and growl to show displeasure. Demonstrate your dominance at such times by height, direct gaze and a low growl. From eight to ten weeks on, carry on with the puppy training as for other puppies but seek canine association as we have indicated. You must control such association as the other dog may not be an ideal companion for yours.

Shipping

Federal regulations state that a puppy may not be shipped by air until he is at least eight weeks old. However, even this isn't a good time because the pup has a fairly high level of anxiety between eight and ten weeks of age.

Quite naturally, new owners want to get their puppy expeditiously and breeders want their pups to get settled in their new homes as soon as possible. Remember that at this age the pup is very nervous. Since this is the period of behavioral refinement in which severe frights and trauma are to be avoided, it's best to wait until the pup is ten weeks old. He will be able to handle the stress much better.

Shipping stress can lead to physical sickness or, at this age, permanent emotional disturbance, putting the eight- to ten-week old puppy in double jeopardy. The stress of travel can lead to a suppression of immunity to disease in a puppy or a dog of any age, which may increase the animal's chances of contracting an infection. This is something you must discuss in detail with your veterinarian. We are more concerned right now, however, in trying to dissuade people from relinquishing puppies to a carrier with no control or knowledge of the emotional trauma the animals might suffer enroute. Often, the effects of the emotional stress of travel aren't recognized as being related to the trip because it can take from two to four days for the problem to surface.

The breed and basic personality of the pup are factors in how the trip affects him. For a pup who has a tendency to be just a little shy, who is not vigorously outgoing, an air freight trip could be devastating.

The shipping kennel should be sturdy with sufficient air movement and not so large that the pup will be tossed around. Most airlines have adequate kennels for sale. Never ship a dog in a wire kennel unless it is covered with heavy canvas. The puppy needs to feel the relative security of the burrowed den, and if he is openly exposed to all of the sights and sounds of a freight depot he could be seriously upset. Leaving the home den is stressful enough without adding to it unnecessarily.

If shipping is necessary, consult with your veterinarian about the requirements for a health certificate and steps you may take to minimize stress and motion sickness.

Transporting by car—Many pups will settle down and ride in a lap nicely. If the pup is really excited, shake him vigorously (but not harshly) by the scruff of the neck, then put him on your lap or on the seat beside you.

If you're driving alone, the puppy might settle down beside you and not be a problem, but be prepared with a covered box or puppy kennel. Put it on the seat beside you and talk to the pup. If a puppy is suddenly removed from his littermates and dumped on the floor of the rear compartment of the car, his resultant fear may affect his emotional development. Furthermore, if he has motion sickness as well, this will make matters worse.

Don't Be Tempted to Keep Two

"If one pup is cute, two are cuter, and besides, they'll keep each other company." Wrong! If you raise two littermates, you're asking for disappointment. To oversimplify, the two pups will form a tight relationship and tune you out. You will never get the response or loyalty from either one that you should. If you're thinking of showing your dog or going into one of the dog sports, neither pup will form the intense communication with you that is necessary for top performance.

There is another reason for not raising littermates together. The more dominant puppy will become consistently more asser-tive and may develop the personality of a bully at the expense of a more submissive puppy who will begin to accept a consistently subordinate attitude as the accepted pattern of behavior. This would be a great disadvantage if the pup were expected to go into competition of any kind when older. It's best to leave the raising of littermates to a professional breeder or trainer who has the facili-ties and time to do a proper job of it.

A similar situation occurs when a pup is raised to maturity with the mother dog. The puppy is not likely to develop the same confident personality as when raised alone or with an unrelated dog. Interestingly, the Guide Dogs for the Blind organization has never had a pup who had been raised with its mother or littermate become a guide dog. Again, it is possible to live happily with a mother-pup pair, but it takes a lot of extra time and effort on the part of the owner in separating them during puppyhood and in providing adequate dog accommodations to facilitate this.

SUMMARY—SUGGESTIONS FOR BREEDERS

There are far too many litters of puppies produced without adequate thought given to the need for socialization and proper handling. If you plan to breed, you can make it a pleasant expe-rience for yourself and insure that the puppies you raise will be well-adjusted, happy pets by planning for the socialization and development in advance. Here are a few things to think about:

1. Don't plan a litter unless you are willing to provide the time and facilities necessary for proper socialization and care.

2. Select breeding stock with sound, well-adjusted personalities from a line of dogs with good temperament.

3. Cull from your breeding program any dogs that produce poor temperament such as shyness, aggression or nervousness in their puppies. Also cull any dogs that exhibit bad behavior traits puppies may learn from association.

4. Spend at least five minutes every other day handling *each* puppy during the critical stage of five to seven weeks.

5. Provide stimulating facilities and toys for the litter. Introduce each puppy to a variety of environments before it leaves for its new home.

6. Sell your puppies between six and eight weeks and avoid placing them in new homes during the critical eighth week if at all possible.

7. Educate your puppy buyers in the proper socialization, training and handling of the puppy and try to assure yourself that the buyer is interested enough to put in the time for this training and socialization before you sign the sales contract.

8. Follow up with your puppy buyers and help them resolve behavioral problems at the onset.

9. Follow up on your line to make sure that personality problems are not showing up in the pups at an older age.

A few simple tests help you get to know the puppy.

It's easy and fun to administer puppy tests, but it's also easy to form snap judgments as a result of the tests. Don't turn puppy testing into more than it is. It's an *indication* of the puppy's natural attitude toward people and a relative measure of the pup's submissiveness and aggressiveness. As such, it's a guide to what type of home and what kind of training will work best. It's *not* a permanent labeling of the pup's adult personality. One reason for this is that environment can play such a large part in the development of a dog's personality.

William E. Campbell developed a series of puppy tests which have become quite popular and which give a consistent overall picture of a puppy's basic emotional behavior. He discusses them in his excellent book, *Behavior Problems in Dogs,* and they are the tests outlined in this chapter.

The score sheet is one we have used for quite some time and lists the reactions we have found to be fairly common. The analysis sheet is a guide to interpreting the results of the testing and incorporates our interpretations of scoring based on observations of the testing we have done. Someday, we hope a controlled study will be conducted on puppy testing and its relevance to the dog's mature personality. Until that time, breeders who use puppy testing tend to develop a sharp eye from experience. They become familiar with the behavior tendencies of their bloodlines and with how certain reactions will develop later in adult dogs. They also can see certain behavior qualities that are not testable, such as that extra spark of smarts or charisma. Some puppies will have a reaction not listed on the score sheet. A pup will not be shy but will be content to observe and quietly do what is indicated but in his own time. This is probably an indication of a slightly more than average independence, or possibly an easy-going, quiet disposition. The pup should be retested another day to make sure the pup wasn't simply just too tired.

The test should be administered by a person who hasn't spent much time with the pups or who is a complete stranger and should be conducted in a room or area that is new to the puppy. These two factors are the means of introducing a puppy's reaction to a stranger and to a new environment into the testing.

Some breeders like to have the prospective buyers of the puppies administer the test when each comes to observe the litter, but other breeders prefer to conduct the test themselves first, scoring each pup in a litter while another person does the actual testing. This gives the breeder an overall view of the behavior of the litter and this information can be helpful when discussing selection with potential new owners.

The breeder might be surprised to discover that a puppy's test score can be quite different from what his litter behavior indicated. A puppy who is very quiet, even to the extent of being picked on by the others, can score as an outgoing people-oriented pup. The reverse can be true also. An assertive pup in the litter might hesitate in associating with a person. Observation of the litter behavior with the other pups can sometimes give a false impression of the pup's innate desire to please and to adjust to people, so it's always advisable for a breeder to puppy-test a litter even though it sometimes might seem unnecessary.

There are a few simple guidelines: The puppies should be awake at the time you go to get them for testing. If you wake a sleeping puppy, the test might not give you a true picture of his reactions. It's also best not to give the test immediately after the pups have eaten. If for any reason you're not sure you got a reliable reaction from any pup, repeat the test the next day.

Testing a puppy isn't a rigid routine that must be followed in an exact pattern. Puppies won't let it be that way. It's simply taking a pup away from its littermates to an area with as few distractions as possible and doing the tests in whatever order seems to work best for each pup.

Here is an example of the way in which a testing routine might be conducted.

Come: Give the pup a few seconds to get oriented to the test area, then call the pup to you by kneeling down and moving your hands in a silent clapping motion. Be sure the pup sees you. If not, move and try again. (Refer to the chart at the end of this chapter for scoring methods.) After the pup has come running to you, do the stroking test.

Stroking Test: Pet the pup from head to tail for 30 seconds. If he bites your hand, he scores an A; if he just mouths your hand and is happily excited, he scores a B.

Notice that the difference between scoring an A and a B is biting. An A score applies to the very aggressive pup. All puppies have needle-sharp teeth and go bounding around with their mouths open, but the pup who scores an A actually nips you. That's his intention though he may not be mean or vicious about it; that's his way of telling you what he thinks.

Come Test

Stroking Test

The Restraint Test: Next, do the restraint test by rolling the puppy on his back and holding him down with your hand on his tummy and between his front legs.

The Following Test: At some point during these few minutes, walk past the pup within a foot or two. If he doesn't follow, walk past again. Be sure he sees you.

If you have trouble getting the pup's attention for the Come or the Following test, do one of the other tests and try again a little later. The important thing is to get a definite reaction from the pup even if it takes several attempts. If you can't get a reaction, that in itself should be recorded as a reaction. Give the pup every opportunity within the few minutes that he is in the test area.

There are two other tests for puppies that are listed but not scored on the score sheet. These can give additional information on the pup's basic behavior tendencies. One is the *toe pinch*. The pup who doesn't feel the pinch will need forceful training. The non-forgiver is not going to be a good obedience trial prospect. The pup who feels the pinch, yipes and then forgives (licking, tail wagging, asking for attention) has a disposition that will be a joy to work with.

Restraint Test

Following Test

Retrieving a knotted sock is an indication of concentration and desire to please. Get the pup's attention by touching his lips with the sock and waving it in his face. Toss it about three feet away. If he goes out to it, he demonstrates he can pay attention to an object. If he brings it back to you, he has a strong desire to please. Some pups might have trouble concentrating at six weeks of age but should be able to by seven weeks. This test isn't for retrievers only. It's a good one to include for many of the working breeds.

The tests are not always the whole story. There's always the puppy who doesn't fit into any one of the scoring categories. All one can do is score the pup as best he can and then use observations to round out the analysis.

Notes and Observations

Notes can be as important as the test scores. We can attest to the vital role of note taking. One author was looking for an assertive pup who could take a lot of hard work and training but who also had a strong desire to please. Her pick-of-the-litter selection had been narrowed down to two puppies with identical scores on the puppy test. However, her notes told her that puppy one had come to her on the first *come* test even though it was distracted by a frayed rug corner. Puppy two needed three "Comes." Her early records showed puppy one was the only puppy who didn't cry when removed from the litter and put on a cement floor at three and a half weeks of age and who was the most investigative pup with a rapidly wagging tail. This cinched the selection but she never would have remembered if she hadn't written notes.

The puppy-testing session is an excellent opportunity for making general observations under conditions that are the same for all the puppies. What is each pup's reaction to you and to the surroundings? Is he generally very curious and active or is he hesitant? Does he whine a lot? Is he easily frightened by a noise or strange object? Write down all the observations. It's amazing how easy it is to forget the little details when observing several puppies.

This type of general observation is a good way of acquainting potential owners with the pups in a litter who might otherwise not be interested in conducting the puppy test themselves. For these people, the breeder can point out the more cautious pups from the more aggressive ones and can also casually incorporate the follow test and the come test into the observation. In the final analysis, the selection of a puppy is probably more emotional than logical. However, it's best to try to place the pup in the home that his natural personality fits best. Many future problems can be prevented this way. A very assertive person will quickly lose patience with a quiet puppy who scores C's and D's (see scoring chart) and a shy person will probably never be able to become the pack leader of a very aggressive dog.

PUPPY BEHAVIOR TEST
SCORE SHEET

(Circle one item in each group)

COME (Attraction to people)	Puppy # 1	2	3	4	5	6
Comes rapidly, nipping at hand	A	A	A	A	A	A
Comes happily, may lick hand, jump in lap	B	B	B	B	B	B
Comes slowly but willingly	C	C	C	C	C	C
Comes very hesitantly, or shyly sits and watches	D	D	D	D	D	D
Doesn't come, may look at you and go his own way	E	E	E	E	E	E

STROKING (Attitude toward social activities)						
Very excited, bites, growls	A	A	A	A	A	A
Jumps and paws, happily	B	B	B	B	B	B
Squirms and licks hand	C	C	C	C	C	C
Rolls over or slinks away	D	D	D	D	D	D
Walks away and stays away	E	E	E	E	E	E

FOLLOWING (Desire to stay in a social environment)						
Pounces on feet, bites pantleg, underfoot	A	A	A	A	A	A
Follows happily, underfoot	B	B	B	B	B	B
Follows slowly but willingly	C	C	C	C	C	C
Doesn't follow, slinks away or sits shyly	D	D	D	D	D	D
Doesn't follow, more interested in going elsewhere	E	E	E	E	E	E

RESTRAINT (Acceptance of human dominance)						
Struggles fiercely, bites, growls	A	A	A	A	A	A
Struggles then settles, or wiggles the whole time	B	B	B	B	B	B
Settles, then struggles	C	C	C	C	C	C
No struggle	D	D	D	D	D	D
Wiggles occasionally	E	E	E	E	E	E

RETRIEVING (Concentration and desire to please)

PINCH (Pain tolerance and forgiveness)

*E in the score indicates a degree of independence. Three E's is a very independent puppy. (Puppy should be retested.) Doesn't require a lot of human companionship. Has very little desire to please. Training requires much repetition and patience from owner.

ANALYSIS OF PUPPY TEST

Extremely shy		Strong desire to please in this range				Extremely aggressive	
3 or more exaggerated "D" responses	3 or more "D" responses	3 or more "C" responses with 1 "D"	3 or more "C" responses with 1 "B"	3 "B" responses with 1 "C"	4 "B" responses	3 "B" responses with "A's"	4 exaggerated "A" responses
Shies away for no reason. Retest 2 times to verify. This pup is virtually untrainable. 2 or 3 "D" responses with 1 or 2 "A's" is a potential fear biter.	Highly submissive. Will not socialize easily. Needs much gentle but firm training and confidence building over long period of time. Not good for young children.	Needs much praise and confidence building. Not good for an impatient person. Good with elderly and handicapped.	Good with children. Good for the inexperienced trainer, will let you make a lot of mistakes.	Outgoing & fairly dominant. Fits in most homes. Very people oriented. Very eager to please but needs a firm hand or will make a pest of himself	Learns quickly and needs firm, consistent training but not harsh physical training.	Contests for pack leadership. Makes a good watchdog. Can be trained into a faithful family dog with consistent repetition in training and minimum of physical punishment.	Will not socialize. Not good with children. Untrustworthy around strangers. Needs special training with very experienced dominant trainer.

*For evaluation of E scores, see footnote on previous page.

CHAPTER 6
SOCIALIZATION CONTINUES
(Eight to Twelve Weeks of Age)

A puppy's two most important needs during the eighth to twelfth weeks are:
- **exposure to a variety of environments**
- **building of self-confidence**

An EEG normally shows adult brain waves in an eight-week old puppy. This tells us that whatever activity a puppy participates in is being recorded by the central nervous system and is going into the puppy's data bank. This is why we say that the manner in which you treat your puppy now will have an effect on his future behavior.

By this age, many puppies have arrived at their new homes. If a puppy stays with the breeder beyond eight weeks of age, it will be a time-consuming process for the breeder because each puppy *must* be given a great deal of individual attention and exposure to different environments.

If you're a potential new owner and are considering buying an older puppy, be certain to acquire the puppy from a conscientious breeder who has taken the time to continue the socialization process beyond the first seven weeks. Puppies who are ignored and left in a kennel to grow until their show quality can be determined, or who are just the last to be sold, are prime candidates for being kennel shy. These pups past twelve weeks of age find it very difficult to form a strong attachment to a person and are more difficult to train because of their shyness (which is basically a result of a lack of self-confidence). However, if a pup has been given sufficient individual time and a variety of experiences, he can become a good addition to the family even when acquired past the age of twelve weeks.

The same conditions apply when a puppy is brought to his new home during the ideal age of six to eight weeks. If this pup is stashed away in a pen and ignored, except for feeding and an occasional romp around the yard, until he's "old enough to learn something," he'll also have kennel-shy symptoms and will be much more difficult to train and to form a close attachment with when older.

VARIETY OF ENVIRONMENT

If there's any possibility that you might show your dog, enter obedience trials, or participate in sled-racing or one of the various types of field trials, this environmental stage of the puppy's development is *vitally* important. Without a variety of experiences at this stage, the pup may not gain the basic attitude necessary to perform adequately in unfamiliar areas away from home. If he isn't introduced to different areas, he may end up being a back-yard genius—perfectly brilliant at home but not worth a nickel anyplace else.

Giving your pup different experiences is important to personality development even if he's going to be a house dog who seldom leaves home. His experiences give him a basis of confidence on which to build a mature personality. If the pup knows only the back yard, he needs to take a walk out front, in a field, in a school yard on Sundays, or to a friend's or neighbor's home. A variety of different areas close to home will be satisfactory. It's important to remember that the pup goes through a fearful stage at eight weeks of age and so he should not be taken to any place of loud noises and confusion during that week.

Ideally, a puppy should be exposed to at least three different environments during these weeks. If the area is such that the puppy can be off the leash, that's great. At this age, he'll probably not wander too far away from you, but if his nose begins to carry him on and on, get his attention and call him back to you by clapping your hands, turning and running, or bending down on your knee. Even though most of the time is spent free-running, this time can also be used for a short session of leash training (see

p. 55). Long visits aren't necessary. Fifteen to twenty minutes are sufficient for each visit to a new place.

If the area you're in requires the pup to be on leash, this will mean the puppy will become leash-trained out of necessity. Let him have as much freedom as possible on the leash and don't demand that he walk at your side the whole time. That's not the purpose of these outings.

Taking the pup for walks in different places is a good way of helping a dog learn to accept new experiences and to trust what his senses tell him. This will help him to adjust to being a dog in a man's world.

BUILDING SELF-CONFIDENCE

The more confidence a pup has, the more quickly he learns. It's easy to build confidence. Talk to your pup. Tell him how good he is (when he is good). Keep him with you as much as possible. You don't have to fuss with him or play with him all the time. In fact, it's best not to, but it's extremely important that he not be isolated for long periods of time, that he can sit on your feet while you're peeling potatoes or lie beside your chair when you're reading the paper. Then if he wanders about the room and gets into mischief, you'll be able to correct him on the spot so that he'll be learning how to please you as well as what does not please you. This learning how to act around people is all part of acquiring a feeling of self-confidence.

Some people say their pup is too wild to be allowed in the house, but this is often a result of the vicious circle. The pup is wild in the house because he's so excited. If he is allowed to be in the house most of the time that you're home and if you keep an eye on him to distract him from mischievous activities, he'll soon learn how to behave nicely.

An excellent means of building self-confidence in a puppy is to spend time alone with him, playing with him, grooming him and beginning to teach him behaviors that are important to you such as to sit, to come and to walk along beside you.

Grooming

Brushing can certainly be included in the puppy's routine by this time. Begin very gradually. Thirty seconds is long enough to have the puppy standing (relatively still) while you brush him.

Praise him just when you were able to accomplish a couple of brush strokes as well as at the end of the grooming session. This is very important because the puppy must know when he has pleased you. Gradually increase the length of time you work with the pup. You'll notice a slow, steady improvement in the cooperation of the puppy. If you've timed your praise well, the pup will realize that grooming is a pleasant experience to be shared with you even though tangles might occasionally complicate the situation.

While you work with your pup, tell him how handsome he is and how well he's behaving. Building his confidence is very important, whether he's going to become a show dog, an obedience or field trial dog or an important member of the family.

If you're wishy-washy in your attitude toward grooming and toward having the pup stand still for a few seconds, your pup will sense this. He will take advantage of you and never stand still. In this case, you'd better read the chapter on molding behavior. You might have to give the pup a scruff shaking to make him realize you're the boss.

Teaching the young puppy to stand will help with combing and brushing.

INTRODUCE THE PUPPY TO TRAINING ACTIVITIES

Building self-confidence and teaching a pup to do different things become a round-robin situation. The more confidence a puppy has, the better he learns and, by the same token, when a puppy is learning to do new things, he is also gaining more confidence in himself and his abilities.

Members of the Guide Dog for the Blind organization found that they could improve their success ratio by giving simple training sessions to their pups from the ages of eight to twelve weeks. Not only do they use these training activities to evaluate the puppies, but they also feel they help assure the puppy the best possible start toward being a guide dog. This is one reason they keep puppies in their puppy-testing program until eleven or twelve weeks of age before sending them to foster homes for a year. We are foolish if we don't take advantage of this fact, one of the many valuable pieces of information which shows up in the analysis of the Guide Dog for the Blind program.

It should be emphasized that this type of puppy activity is not a rigid, militaristic regime in which a misstep is punished. This is not the way to build confidence. We're working with emotionally immature animals susceptible to fears and confidence-destroying tactics similar to those that affect the human child. Therefore, perhaps "training" is not the best word to use. The term "pre-training" might better indicate the intent of these activities— assuming that such a term does not belittle the importance of the activities because we assure you that these activities at this age will pay big dividends in the learning attitudes of your dog when he is older.

A Sample Session

Take the puppy to whatever room or yard area you choose. At first the puppy can be carried and then, after the first few sessions, taken to the area on a leash. It's important to remember that at this age you're showing the puppy what you want him to do. He may not respond with a good performance until it's been repeated numerous times.

Don't start teaching the pup to "stay" at this age because you will have to correct him even if only a gentle push back when he moves from his position. He'll totally misunderstand this, will take it as punishment and won't know why he's being punished.

We like to begin working with the "Sits" because this is a formal exercise. It is best if the puppy is fresh. Use whichever "Sit" method works best for you and your pup. One popular method is the jacknife procedure. Put one hand on the puppy's chest, call his name and say "Sit" while you jacknife the puppy into a sitting position by pushing back on his chest and forward on the rear of the puppy's stifle joint. Repeat this two or three times. The puppy is going to be wiggling, so you'll have to practice your coordination and do it quickly. Don't make the puppy stay sitting yet. That comes later. Another way of teaching the pup to sit is to use the conditioning method, a good means of getting the pup to pay attention to you that may be preferable for people who have trouble getting their hands on a wiggling puppy (see p. 99 for this method.)

The next activity in the session is the "Come" exercise, done much the same way as in the puppy test except that now you verbally call the puppy to come to you. Position yourself several feet away from the puppy. Kneel or bend down and say "Rover, come," at the same time you are clapping your hands. Repeat this several times if necessary to get the puppy to come to you. As the puppy begins to understand this exercise, and as you begin to get his attention more easily, move back a few feet farther. Just don't make the mistake of calling him from a distance of twenty-five or thirty yards when he's not paying attention to you. If you do that and he ignores you, you're teaching him that it's okay to ignore you. You're defeating the purpose of puppy pre-training, which is to pattern him to pay attention to you and to do what you ask of him. (Later on, when you are asking much more of him, this pattern will pay great dividends.)

Another excellent activity which should be included in these sessions is "Fetch" training. Even if you have a breed that isn't a retriever, fetching is a great thing for the puppy to learn. It's not only an easy and pleasant way to exercise a dog but is also the basis for many other tasks the dog can learn in the future such as carrying the newspaper. (Another excellent way of giving a dog self-confidence is training him to do things for you.)

Teaching retrieving is easy and fun if you don't expect perfect performance the first few times. Remind yourself that this won't come naturally to all pups at first, especially the very independent and the very shy pups. But keep at it. The rewards are great. The younger you begin teaching this, the easier it will be.

Tie a sock or small cloth (white or light color) in a knot. Dangle it excitingly in front of the pup's mouth. Encourage him if he starts to lick it or opens his mouth. Toss the sock a couple of feet in front of the pup. If he goes to it and sniffs, praise him like crazy! If he picks it up, attract his attention to come back to you by calling him, clapping your hands, patting the floor or whatever will entice him to return. Don't overdo—two or three retrieves at a time is plenty. If he's not too excited about it, once is enough. Gradually increase the length of your throw. If the pup reaches the point where he picks it up and runs away, put a cord or string on his collar and gently guide him back to you. Some people prefer using a small ball. The movement is a good attention-getter. Just be sure that you don't throw the ball too far to get the pup's attention.

Margaret Pearsall suggests using a brightly colored ball and rolling it off his nose from the top of his head. If the movement of the ball doesn't interest the pup, face him close to a wall so that the ball will roll back out towards the pup again.

The first two or three times, *leash training* will be done at the conclusion of the session. Put the leash on the puppy when you begin to walk him back to his familiar home area. After doing this a couple of times, you can also take the puppy to his training area on leash if it isn't too far. Introduce the pup to the leash by using as lightweight a one as possible (never chain!). Attach it to a narrow buckle-type collar, checked often to be certain it's not getting too small.

Some pups will get very excited on a leash. This is one reason we suggest putting it on just shortly before returning to the familiar home-bed area. He'll be more intent on returning to a familiar place. Then there's the puppy who will try to eat the leash. Encourage him to pay attention to you by coaxing with your voice and patting your leg as you walk. Keep the puppy moving at a brisk pace, almost a run, and you should be able to keep his attention.

CHAPTER 7
PUPPY GOES TO A NEW HOME

"Enjoy getting acquainted with your dog, but don't expect too much too soon."

Nothing equals the excitement of anticipating a new puppy! The fun of bringing a pup home and introducing him to his new family is a very special experience. What hopes we have for our perfect puppy! He will, of course, become a well-mannered dog, staying quietly at our side, eager to follow our every command. Well, it's a long road from the cuddly puppy to the mature dog, but with some effort and understanding it can be traveled successfully. It all begins with Day One in the new home.

The first few days a puppy is in his new home can be trying for both the puppy and the new owner because both are trying to adjust to a new situation. After all, the puppy finds he has been suddenly taken from his den and littermates and is expected to immediately accept a new, foreign way of life. However, with patience and a sense of humor on the part of the new owner, the first few days can be accomplished with good feelings on both sides.

Breeders and behaviorists generally agree that seven weeks of age (forty-nine days) is the ideal age for a puppy to go to his new home, with six to eight weeks being the most desirable age range. The six- to eight-week old puppy still needs a lot of rest and will take morning and afternoon naps. For the first day or two, however, he might be very excited and spend much of the day in motion, checking out his new home. As long as he isn't hurting himself or anything else in the environment, let him investigate wherever and whatever takes his fancy.

If the puppy is eight weeks old when he first comes home, be very patient with him. This is the fear period and sharp noises or harsh treatment will leave him with fear which may take months to overcome. Let him take his time getting acquainted with every-thing and don't take him to places where he will be subjected to loud and frightening sounds or activities. If at all possible, trips to the veterinarian should be arranged either before or after the eighth week.

If the puppy is ten to twelve weeks old when you first bring him home, he'll be more rambunctious, especially if he's one of the larger breeds, and he'll sleep considerably less during the day. However, he's at an age where you can get his attention quite easily and where he'll want to please you and stay close to you. It's very important that the puppy's pre-training activities should begin now (see p. 53).

Some puppies get excited and will pull on the leash. Use your voice and a fast pace to get the pup's attention.

THE FIRST DAY

Before the puppy arrives at your home, we assume you will have made adequate preparations, such as a bed with a blanket or a piece of carpet in it (a cardboard box works fine for this). Know where the puppy will be kept when you're absent from home during the day (back yard, kennel or a puppy-proof room), know where you want the puppy to urinate and defecate, and have a supply of puppy food on hand and a food and a water bowl. You will be much more relaxed if you have thought these things out before the puppy arrives.

The main concern with the first couple of days is in letting the pup get acquainted. Within the area where he is allowed to roam, he should be given much time on his own to sniff and explore, to find his bed area, to determine good nap-taking spots, etc. (See the section on house-training for the beginning of those activities.)

If the puppy is going to be kept in a pen area for a certain amount of time each day, be certain he has a few toys available (p. 26), and be certain that he won't be left for long periods of time. The ideal situation is for a puppy to be with someone a good bit of the time for the first week or two. The best time to initiate a puppy into your life, especially if the family is working or in school most of the day, is to arrange for the puppy's arrival during a period when someone will be home on vacation, at least for the first several days of the puppy's arrival.

Even though short play periods with the puppy are fun, the puppy doesn't need to be played with constantly (in fact, preferably not) but the pup does need to learn who his people are and what are the limits of his territory. You can begin, even at six to eight weeks of age, to show the puppy where he can go and what he can do, and that no, he may not chew on the chair leg. Most puppies are easily directed by your voice as described in the chapter on molding behavior. But occasionally a puppy can be either very stubborn or overly active. Don't allow yourself to reach the point of irritation where you slap or spank the puppy. It's preferable to give the puppy a short but firm scruff shake (p. 71). This is a very effective form of discipline. If you find yourself using severe discipline more than a couple of times during the first week, you'd better evaluate your attitude toward the puppy.

Maybe you don't really want to have one around. This attitude, even though suppressed, certainly isn't conducive to raising a happy, well-behaved dog.

The most difficult part of the puppy's first day is the first night in a new and strange place. This subject deserves a section of its own.

FIRST NIGHT ALONE

The puppy's first night alone in his new home can be one of intense fear. The fear of suddenly being left alone can lead to anxiety which can show up later as a behavior problem such as excessive barking or digging at the carpet.

There aren't many alternatives for a pup's first night and it is certain to be a stressful experience to some degree, but there is one method that works very well. Let the puppy spend his first couple of nights in the bedroom of his new master. Put a box in the room

Keeping the puppy in the bedroom the first two nights makes the adjustment to a new home much easier for both the pup and the people.

with a blanket or carpet in it or just put the bedding on the floor beside your bed. The pup might ignore your efforts and select his own place, like under the bed or in a corner. Let the pup stay wherever he will relax and settle down.

A puppy is usually exhausted by nighttime and will sleep through the night. If not, a hand reaching down in the dark helps to calm him. (If this doesn't work, you'd better get up and take the pup out to urinate.) First thing in the morning, carry the pup outdoors or to the area covered with newspapers. You usually will have to carry him because he might not be able to walk as far as that by himself without urinating until he's ten to twelve weeks old.

Two nights, or sometimes three, is usually enough of this special treatment. By then the pup should be ready to accept his bed in the regular place you have selected for him. If you don't plan to allow the pup to continue sleeping in your room it's best not to let him stay past the third night. If you wait much past that time, the pup will reach a point where he won't want to be moved and you'll be back where you started with the crying. If these special measures aren't possible, you had better buy some ear plugs and be prepared for loud crying for at least two nights.

You may want to consider allowing the puppy to continue sleeping in the bedroom. If you work and are away from home a lot, this is one way of giving your dog a sense of your presence and of your desire to be with him as much as possible.

If you decide to do this you should keep the pup in a metal wire kennel during the night (see p. 63) or put the pup on a short rope tied to a leg of the bed until he's house-trained, with his own bedding there also, of course. The rope should be short enough to allow him to lie down without getting tangled.

HOUSE-TRAINING

People have a tendency to get very excited over the process of house-training. What's needed are a realistic philosophy, a lot of paper towels and some carpet deodorant. Life is a lot simpler with linoleum and vinyl floors, but this seems to be the age of carpets.

As explained in the discipline section, spanking does more harm than good and this is especially true in house-training.

Many puppies react negatively to spanking. This can create additional problems, often actually prolonging the training procedure. The least painful approach for both the owner and the pup is to establish a routine and to praise the puppy for performance at the proper time in the proper place.

One important routine is to feed the puppy at the same times every day and when he's finished eating, immediately take him to the area you have selected for his urination and defecation. Wait for him to do his chores, then praise him. The praise is the secret to house-training. It shows the puppy what you want him to do and where. It's a good idea to associate a command with the house-breaking, such as "Do your business." A dog will learn to respond and it's very nice to have a dog who will empty on command, which is especially important when traveling.

Have you ever put a puppy outdoors, left him there for fifteen to twenty minutes, then let him in again only to have him immediately make a puddle or a pile on the carpet? It's very easy to believe he's doing this on purpose, and it's very easy to get very angry. However, the pup simply doesn't have it all figured out yet. For one reason or another, he's still confused about the indoor-outdoor situation. Besides that, he doesn't urinate and defecate until he has the urge, and he didn't happen to get the urge until he was in on the carpet. It's going to take some time on your part to help him get the whole procedure straightened out. Some puppies learn in a few days, some not until they're three and four months old. Some puppies simply don't have the muscle control until they're several months old.

Go outdoors with the pup and stand around and wait. If the pup doesn't do anything, give up and return to the house with the puppy. Take him back out every five or ten minutes until he urinates or defecates. When he does, praise him! It may take several days of dedicated effort before the pup begins to realize what you want him to do but he will gradually understand and his body will also gradually adjust to a time schedule. This procedure is especially trying for the person with a winter puppy in a cold climate, but it's effective. It does work.

Always take the puppy out after meals, immediately after he awakens from a nap and after a play period, or even in the middle of a play period if it's a long and vigorous one. Between times, watch for signs—some pups suddenly get restless and begin to act nervous; some start going in circles. Rush the pup to his outside place immediately, even if you have to carry him. If the pup has an accident, quickly take him to the yard or paper area. You can scold the pup if you catch him in the act, but no spanking! Just rushing him to the acceptable place will startle him quite sufficiently.

Even after you and your pup have worked out a routine, there will still be an occasional accident in the house. Clean it up, use a carpet deodorizer available in pet shops (or use one part white vinegar to four parts water) and be patient.

There's a good dog reason for deodorizing spots on the floor. When a puppy gets a whiff of that particular odor, an eliminative reflex is set off and thereafter he does what is natural for him. This odor works to your advantage in training him for one certain area such as one section of the yard, provided you can keep the scent off other areas.

If you are gone during the day and the puppy is kept in the house, he should be confined to a room that's easy to clean and is mostly covered with newspapers. Gradually decrease the space covered by paper to only one small area, but don't begin this process for at least one week. If he uses the newspaper while you're there with him, reward him with a pat and a "good puppy." At this age it's difficult to train for outdoors and for paper both because the puppy doesn't understand the connection between the paper and the yard. When he is older, probably by three months, you can remove the papers and train him for outdoors only.

CRATES AND KENNELS

Another means of controlling the puppy so he doesn't have accidents when you're not home is to train him to stay in a wire crate. As with everything else in puppy training, this is done gradually. Have the crate always available, leaving the door open. Drop pieces of his food inside and he'll quickly become very comfortable with going in to eat the pieces. Use it as his bed if possible. You can feed him in it. When you first close the door, stay there with him, talking to him. Open it after a few minutes and praise him, even if he did make a fuss. It will gradually become his "place" and he'll feel very secure in it.

The puppy shouldn't be confined continuously (except at night), but a crate can be a big help for an hour or two at a time. As the pup grows older, he can spend longer periods of time in a crate as long as it isn't a regular long-term arrangement. Crates are also excellent for car travel. It keeps the dog safe from sudden stops and swerves, and it keeps the people safe from an excitable dog.

There's nothing cruel about using a crate. It's very natural for a dog because it fits into his den concept. Most dogs who have their own crates consider them a place of security. The only conceivable problems arise if the pup is forced into the cage suddenly and becomes frightened or if he is left in it for hours at a time and becomes excessively lonely and bored.

Some families find a back yard kennel or pen area a necessity for confining the dog to a particular area of the yard. This offers protection for flowers and landscaping during the puppy's rambunctious growing-up months or when the puppy is left outdoors with no people present. These can be made of chain link and can be an attractive area, easy to keep clean.

Care must be taken, however, not to put the puppy in his kennel and then forget about him. Everyone in the twentieth century is busy, but if you're too busy to have the puppy out of the kennel everyday to be with you in the house or in the yard, then you're too busy to have a dog. Yard kennels are a convenience if used properly but should never be considered for twenty-four hour a day confinement.

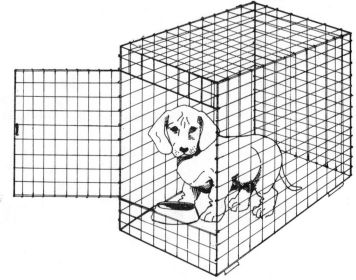

The crate is a very helpful way to control the puppy for short periods of time.

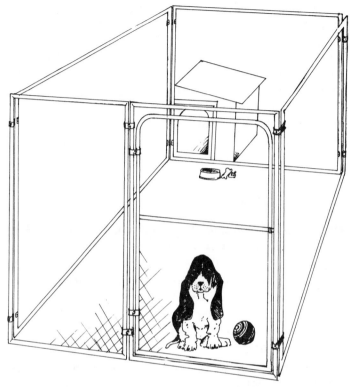

A pen keeps the pup from destroying plants in the yard but the puppy should be trained and played with every day.

PLAY

Puppies do love to play! It's easy to overlook the importance of play and to assume it's just something puppies do. Actually, play is very important and is part of the maturing process. A puppy learns what his abilities are by playing. It sharpens the senses of sight and scent. Play also stimulates the brain, keeping the pup alert and interested in his environment. Don't forget, it's the alert puppy who learns quickly.

Play can be as simple as a running game—inviting the pup by giving the canine signal for play, a play-bow, putting your hands on your knees and bending over. Take a quick step and the pup will probably start running around you in a circle. Retrieving is a great game that can be used for exercise as the pup grows older. See p. 45 for teaching the puppy how to retrieve, which should be done at this age.) Tug-of-war is *not* a good game for most puppies because it encourages aggressiveness and mouthiness.

You can encourage play by seeing that the pup has a variety of toys available. A ball of proper size is excellent. The rolling ball is chased and pounced upon and hunted out as prey. Other toys can be as varied as your imagination as long as they're safe. A sock, an old canvas shoe, a rawhide bone are a few ideas. Pet stores also have an interesting variety of toys.

PUPPIES AND OLDER DOGS

Young puppies should never be left alone with older dogs unless you *know* beyond a doubt how the older dog treats rambunctious youngsters. There's a good reason for this. Puppies don't begin to show submissiveness until they're about four months of age. Until they reach that point, they don't have an ounce of sense around older dogs and will usually pester them until the dog puts a stop to it. This might be done in a manner that doesn't injure a dog, such as scruff shaking or snapping and growling. However, it might also be done with a bite that can injure a small puppy seriously. Don't take that chance.

By the time the puppy is four months old the risk of injury becomes much less. The pup begins to assume the submissive posture of rolling on his side when threatened by an older dog and this acts as a damper on the situation. A puppy at least four months old knows enough to move out of the way quickly, too.

CHAPTER 8
SHAPING YOUR PUP'S BEHAVIOR

"Barring extremes of shyness or aggressiveness, there is enough potential variation of behavior patterns that you'll be able to modify your puppy's behavior to fit in with your lifestyle. You do this by encouraging the characteristics that you like."

If every pup in the United States lived up to his potential, we would soon have a population of perfect canids. But thanks to us humans, only a small percentage of pups end up being ideal dogs. One reason for this is the little-understood fact that much of a puppy's future behavior is set by what he experiences between three and fourteen weeks of age. His basic attitude toward people and his desire to please are established during these weeks.

This chapter will discuss the many possibilities the breeder and new owner have to mold the behavior of their pup to fit into the family lifestyle. The subjects discussed in this chapter don't necessarily pertain only to the first three to four months, but this is the age when the owner and the pup's environment are both having a very strong influence in the development of the puppy's mature personality.

BEGIN NOW

It comes as a surprise to most people that their puppy is beginning to learn how to behave from the day he enters his new home. An example of this is in teaching the puppy to sit for his feed dish.

Hold the food dish up. The instant the pup's rear moves in a sitting direction, say "Sit" and immediately get the dish to the floor. The first few times you try this the pup may not look like he's going to sit. Try to time the food dish delivery with a bending of his hind legs. After several days of good timing on your part, the pup will be sitting when he sees you with the food dish. This is an example of how easily a pup's behavior can be molded. Beginning as early as seven weeks of age.

Conditioning the pup to sit is also an example of how the dog's behavior and attitudes are being shaped. A pup can just as easily be conditioned to bite your pantleg or to bark at you. If your response is picking him up and holding him in an effort to stop the behavior, the pup perceives it as a reward (even though unintentional on your part) and therefore sees the behavior as acceptable.

A puppy's behavior is constantly being molded all day long in this same manner. Whenever we praise the pup, pat or cuddle him, that behavior is being encouraged. Whenever we speak sharply or distract the pup or scruff shake, that behavior is being discouraged. Puppies develop habits very quickly. If you can control *your* behavior and pay attention to what actions you're rewarding, you're going to end up with a nice dog you'll be happy to have around. It's much easier to encourage good behavior than to change bad behavior after the puppy has been allowed to get away with it.

DISCIPLINE

You can enjoy your puppy, relax and have lots of fun while at the same time setting limits and boundaries for his behavior. Before an owner can effectively discipline a pup, it helps to have some knowledge of basic canine behavior. This includes an understanding of the social structure of the group that the puppy will be living with. In any group in the canine world there *must* be a pack leader. A dog is always willing to take this role himself any time you become wishy-washy or too lenient. (The role of the pack leader is discussed in detail in Chapter 10.) Your role as pack leader begins when you bring the puppy home, and it is a matter, at this age, of your attitude and approach to discipline.

The pup's social attraction to you during the first three months is very strong. Negative discipline such as slapping or hitting with a newspaper works *against* the pup's natural attraction to people. This type of discipline can build a wall of defense mechanisms on the part of the pup that will result in a dog much more difficult to train and to communicate with when he's older.

Your pup has to *learn* what good behavior is. He's not born knowing your opinion about such things as chewing shoes or jumping up on children. He has to learn your definition of good behavior before he can comprehend bad behavior. If all you do is screech, holler and spank, you're going to have another one of the many crazy mixed-up dogs that exist to damage the dog's reputation as a species. The poor pup will only know what makes you angry. He won't know what makes you happy because you've never shown him, so he does strange things in frustration like frantically digging holes and tearing pillows.

The first rule in puppy discipline is for you to become the pack leader and to teach the pup what behaviors you like and don't like. When the pup is sitting or lying at your feet instead of chewing your shoe or trying to leap in your lap, tell him he's a good pup; give him a pat. If this excites him, get him settled down again. After awhile he'll learn how to accept your praise. Some dogs do best with vocal praise only. If your pup is a little on the hyper side he might be one of these, but give him a couple weeks' trial first. Just one or two pats at a time is sufficient, preferably on the chest or shoulder (the choice of many trainers). Don't overdo it! Constantly petting the puppy is as bad for him as never touching or talking to him at all. An indulged puppy is spoiled and never grows up.

A means of calming your pup and rewarding him at the same time is to take your middle finger and scratch him in the center area of his chest. Try it. You'll be amazed at how he'll stand quietly and enjoy it.

Correction followed by praise works very well in teaching the puppy not to jump on people. When he jumps on you, either push him down with your knee or grab him by the scruff of the neck and hold him down on the ground on his own four feet. Then pat him and tell him how good he is for standing on the ground. The pup will catch on quickly if you consistently say "NO" when he starts to jump on you and praise him immediately when he is on the ground (he may be wiggling and bouncing around, but if he's not jumping on you, praise him). Visitors and other family members must do the same thing so that the pup will learn this quickly and thoroughly.

The second rule in puppy discipline is to distract the pup when he gets into mischief. Distraction is another means of showing your puppy which actions you do and don't like. It's a relatively slow process but it's easy to do and is amazingly effective over a period of time. For example, use your voice, "Hey!" or a loud sound like a hand clap, or point your finger at the pup. Often one of these will work to divert the pup's attention. Don't overuse "NO," however. If spoken constantly it becomes a nagging sound to the pup and he soon tunes it out. Save it for serious misbehavior.

When your pup begins chewing on the piano leg, get his attention quickly. Clap your hands or holler "Hey!" Try to get him to come to you. If you're not more attractive to him than the piano leg, pick him up and carry him away. When he's in an approved area and being his sweet self again, praise him. Tell him how good he is.

There comes a day, however, when your pup needs more than distraction or a voice command. Every pup in the world needs physical discipline sooner or later. Don't kid yourself into thinking your pup is different. (If he's different at three and four months of age, he won't be at seven and eight months of age. Believe us!)

The third rule in puppy discipline is—DON'T LET YOUR PUP BECOME AN OBNOXIOUS DOG. Use a more severe discipline than your voice when the situation requires it. For the times when your puppy is being a real stinker and your impulse is to spank or hit him, scruff shaking is a very good thing to do instead. Timing is important for this. The action must be quick and firm. The puppy must know that you mean it. If he thinks you're giving him a vigorous scratching on his neck or behind his ear, you've lost that round.

Scruff shaking is a canine form if discipline. An older bitch will use it on an obnoxious puppy. The bitch will grab the pup's scruff and whip him from one side to the other side and back again. End of discipline. We needn't be quite that vigorous. Two or three shakes strong enough to make the front legs move are

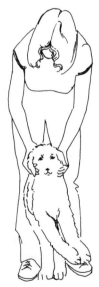

Scruff shaking is a dog-language discipline and is preferable to spanking.

usually effective. As your puppy grows older and larger, especially if he's a big breed, you will want to use both hands, one on each side of the neck, and lift the pup's front feet off the ground.

A more impressionable form of disciplining and of demonstrating your leadership role is to roll the dog over on his side and then lean over his shoulder and head, shaking his scruff while kneeling beside him. This should be used only on the strong-willed or assertive dog.

If you've used this form of discipline you know what a good means it is. If you haven't used it before, you'll probably be glad to know of it. It's another means of establishing your dominance as pack leader. Again, though, don't overuse it but when you do use it, make sure it's a strong correction.

If the pup is misbehaving badly enough to need a scruff shaking, the discipline should not be followed by praise—for example, when you catch him in the act of destroying a chair leg or when he growls at you. Then the discipline must be quickly given and the pup must be ignored for at least fifteen to twenty minutes with no petting or praise. After this period of time you can speak to him quietly but with a firm voice. Whatever you do, don't start apologizing.

BEHAVIOR PROBLEMS

Most behavior problems are caused by boredom and isolation. This is why we say it is essential to spend time every day with your pup and have him with you in the house or the yard while you're home. We've said this earlier, but it bears repeating. If you're too busy to stay home most evenings and associate with your pup, then you're too busy to have a puppy. When you're not home the pup should have some chewable items to work on.

The dog who remains quite troublesome hasn't yet acquired a clear understanding of his relationship with his people. The pack leadership has not yet been firmly established and the pup must learn where his place is in the hierarchical structure within the family. Also, some dogs apparently have the personality type that lends itself to taking every advantage. Be realistic and admit it if this is the case. This pup will just take more consistent effort in the discipline department than another personality might require.

Some pups present a worse chewing problem than others. This indicates that the pup has an oral approach to life. In determining how to go about controlling this, think carefully about how your actions look to the pup when you find him chewing on something. Are you doing anything that could be perceived by him to be a reward? Are you touching him and/or (from his point of view) making a game out of taking the object away such as tug-of-war? Any touching or excessive handling on the body in the attempt to make him stop chewing could be viewed by the pup as pleasant, in other words as a reward, so that in his view of life there is nothing wrong with chewing. Are you distracting him from chewing by giving him a tidbit (which he would perceive as a reward for chewing)?

When you catch your pup in the act of chewing, scold him with a sharp "NO!" or "Stop that!" Shake him by the scruff of the neck. If the pup hasn't dropped the object or you haven't been able to remove it easily, pinch his lip against the biting surface of his teeth. He should open his mouth. When the object is no longer in his mouth, take him away from that place, leading by the collar. At this point he is no longer chewing and is displaying good behavior so after a few minutes give him the "Sit" command and then praise him by telling him that now he's a good dog. The puppy should have chewing toys of his own. Give him one of these.

DON'T OVERINDULGE

In the process of building a feeling of confidence in your pup and of establishing a bond of communication, don't fall into the trap of touching the puppy excessively. This eventually has the effect of telling your dog that you are allowing him to become the pack leader, that the dog's pleasure is your main concern. This results in the dog's not paying attention to you and makes any kind of training very difficult.

Some people have asked about using the stroke versus the pat on their dogs. We believe that there isn't much difference between the two. The important thing here is degree—how much stroking? It's easy to continue stroking a dog because after all the coat is pleasant to the touch and a dog obviously enjoys it tremendously. A dog can easily get the impression that this is his privilege and will insist on being stroked constantly and can become a spoiled brat. A good way to avoid this canine attitude is to give an obedience command preceding a social stroking-play session. "Sit" followed by an "OK" and then a play session really helps to maintain an emotionally healthy dog. Give him a "Sit" before you give him his bowl of food. When using touch as a means of praising the pup for a job well done, many trainers use pats on the chest for praise and occasionally a pat on the shoulder. But there's nothing wrong with a stroke—it's just too easy to overdo it.

PUPPIES WILL BE PUPPIES

There's sometimes the possibility that the new owner will exaggerate the degree of the behavior problem of a puppy. Especially with a first puppy, the owner may not realize that some digging, some chewing, barking and jumping up is very natural behavior. This is why we keep stressing that it's up to the owner to teach the puppy what to do and what not to do. Puppies are canids and there are certain behaviors that are simply not wrong from the puppy's point of view. So don't get angry at the pup just because you decide he should act more like a person than a dog. Simply get busy and show him what you want him to do and what you don't want him to do.

Molding your pup's behavior isn't done in a day or two. It takes weeks of simply praising good behavior and discouraging bad behavior. It's a style of living, a rigorous formal program.

You say your puppy is easy to get along with, responds to you readily and really isn't any trouble to speak of, that your puppy doesn't need to have his behavior molded? Well, if you think this puppy won't change as he grows up, you're sadly mistaken because sweet little puppies always grow into independent dogs with minds and instincts of their own.

Our pet peeve is the person who doesn't see any reason to teach a puppy how to behave. This is often the same person who in a few months decides that the dog is too much of a nuisance and who either puts him in a pen and forgets about him (thereby compounding the bad behavior) or who takes him to the Humane Society moaning that he just can't do a thing with that dog. "He won't pay any attention to me." The myth that a dog's life is a good life isn't necessarily so.

Accept your puppy as he is, not as you think he should be. If your pup is shy, it won't help a bit for you to say, "I forbid you to act that way!" Accept the shyness and do what needs to be done (see Chapter 11). This also applies to the independent puppy and the assertive puppy. Over a period of weeks you'll find that confidence and communication between the two of you are increasing and his general behavior will be changing to fit your desires.

CHAPTER 9
DEVELOPMENT FROM THREE TO SIX MONTHS

This is an age to *enjoy*—but watch out! Your puppy is *not* too good to be true.

The rapid changes noticeable in the puppy's behavior during the first three months have leveled off. The central nervous system is now well-developed. By three months of age the pup's problem-solving ability is functioning well but his immaturity gets in the way. In other words, he has a short attention span and is too rambunctious to settle down and learn complicated behavior. However, he's certainly ready to learn simple commands (as discussed in Chapter 12).

This is a delightful age and passes much too quickly. By the end of this period, the large-breed pups have grown to approximately two-thirds of their mature size and small breeds may be close to their final height. After six months of age the puppy will become much more independent, will reach sexual maturity and will be very responsive to physiological stimuli. However, the age from three to six months is still one of puppy charm and innocence. The pup and people are adjusting to each other and the pup is learning what the pack rules are. He's readily able to cope with life by now, he's a willing worker, and he is happy to try whatever you ask (at least most of the time).

Taking the pup to different places continues to be important at this age. The pup's environmental awareness is at a peak now. He's ready for anything. Exposure to a variety of places will continue to be a factor in building self-confidence in the puppy and will help him take stressful events in the future in his stride.

The second set of teeth begins to appear during this period, which can cause chewing and biting problems. The puppy needs some items of his own for chewing.

DOMINANCE AND SUBMISSION

By four months of age, the pup is beginning to show signs of dominance and submissiveness toward other dogs. Previously we noted that a young puppy shouldn't be left with irritable older dogs because the puppy wouldn't recognize the dominance signs of the older dog and wouldn't respond with a sign of submission. As a consequence the pup might get bitten. However, around four months of age this changes and the pup becomes aware that dominance is displayed by a tail held straight up and tightly moving, by a growl and showing of the front teeth and by the dominant dog's putting his head over the shoulder area of the other dog. The submissive signs that the pup will display toward a dominant dog are a flattening of the ears, tucking the tail between the legs and cowering if not rolling over on the side or back. Usually, a puppy is submissive to an older dog although in some instances a very assertive puppy will soon realize he can be dominant to an especially submissive adult. With young dogs close in age, some pups will be dominant over others, and generally a dominant-submissive relationship is established very quickly. With some pups, it's a change-about situation as they take turns at dominance and submission.

Young dogs display dominance by leaning over the other dog.

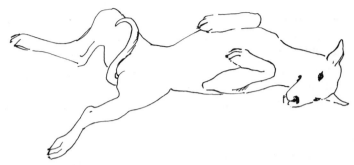

Total submissiveness can be demonstrated to either another dog or a person.

AVOIDANCE PERIOD

Around four months of age the pup will go through an avoidance period similar to the fear period experienced at eight weeks. The puppy becomes very hesitant about doing anything new and different and becomes quite suspicious of anything new that is brought into his home environment or of any new place he might be visiting.

If your pup has a quiet personality, he may not respond as happily during training sessions or he may seem hesitant and a little fearful if you take him to a new place. If this is the case, ease off the training routine. Make it fun; just enjoy being with your pup.

On the other hand, if you have a very independent or assertive pup, this age may find him in a relatively receptive frame of mind. His being a little apprehensive of new things in his life will tend to make him look to you for support. While he's paying attention to you, get busy and teach him something.

A SENSE OF TERRITORY

During these three months, many pups are beginning to acquire a feeling of the family house and/or yard as being their territory. The natural canine tendency is to protect this territory— the aggressiveness of this protective attitude will depend upon the dog's personality and the encouragement he receives when he begins to act protective as a puppy. The problem with encouraging an aggressive puppy to bark and snarl protectively is the lack of control that often accompanies this activity. As the puppy grows older and more aggressive, the owner begins to realize that he can no longer control the dog's aggressiveness. He can't simply stop the dog's protectiveness at any point he desires. For this reason we don't encourage an owner to aim to raise his puppy for a guard dog. This is a very specialized training which requires a great deal of control and should be done by or with experienced trainers. However, for most families, having a dog who will bark at the approach of a stranger to the property is sufficient protection.

Now is the time to decide how much barking you'll put up with and to begin shaping the puppy's behavior toward that goal. If you want the puppy to announce visitors and then stop barking, let him know this. Use a specific word such as "Who's there?" or "Bark," or whatever you might say when someone approaches the house. After the pup has barked a few times and you've acknowledged the person's presence, distract the puppy. The instant he pauses in his barking, praise him and tell him he's a good dog. If you repeat the pattern each time he starts barking, the puppy will soon learn the boundaries of acceptable barking. Obviously, some dogs bark more and longer than others but if you begin conditioning the behavior as young as possible, you should be able to avoid a serious barking problem.

If your puppy doesn't want to stop barking when you think he should, you may need to use a strong distraction such as a sharp sound. Some marbles in a coffee can often startle a puppy to silence—if he's outdoors, throw a bucket of water on him. If you have a real barker, you may want to use a "bark collar" such as the one manufactured by TriTronics in Tucson, Arizona, which activates a sound when the dog barks.

TEETHING

In many breeds there can be retention of puppy teeth during the period that permanent teeth are erupting. This can have a long lasting effect in that the pathway the permanent teeth will take if the puppy teeth are retained will be abnormal and may lead to permanent problems with the way in which the teeth close together. Another problem associated with retention of puppy teeth is damage to the surrounding gum which may progress to chronic oral disease in adult life. Bearing in mind that the pup between four and five months is extra sensitive, you should pay careful attention to the possibility of teething problems and if you have any doubts that teething is not going well, you should consult your veterinarian immediately.

A VETERINARY CHECKUP

Puppies must receive a rabies vaccination from three-to-four months of age although this varies from state to state and with the type of vaccine used. At the beginning of this century rabies was a serious problem in the domestic dog population, which of course meant that humans in intimate association with these dogs were constantly endangered. The incidence of rabies in our dog population now only makes up about four percent of the rabies cases reported each year and there have been only nine cases of human rabies in the last three years, with none in 1980. On the other hand, the incidence of rabies in the wildlife population around our cities is on the increase. Rabies is out there and there can be no doubt that the only reason it is not affecting our dog population seriously and that practically no human cases have occurred recently is due in large measure to the extensive and sound rabies programs for our domestic pets.

Depending on the schedule you have with your veterinarian, your pup may be receiving the last shot in the distemper series at this age also. This is a good time to have your puppy checked by your veterinarian for internal parasites and for general health progress.

THE END OF PUPPYHOOD

By the end of the fifth month the pup is entering his adolescence and is acquiring mature personality traits. Many pups now begin to assert their independence, sometimes to the point of seeming to appear to be deaf and blind. Don't let him bluff you. You *are* the pack leader, aren't you? The next chapter will give you a good understanding of this concept.

To summarize the three to six month age period, the most important help you can give your puppy is to let him know you're the pack leader so that there's no doubt in his mind. The loyalty shown by the dog to his master and family is a manifestation of pack behavior. You and your family are the pack to which your dog belongs and the house and yard are his den and territory.

SUMMARY

What your puppy should know:

You are the pack leader.
You must be paid attention to.
You have house rules which must be learned.

What you should know:

No tug-of-war games	This encourages aggressiveness.
No "sic em" games	This encourages rough play that can get out of control. Dogs should not be encouraged to attack smaller animals.
No excessive touching and handling	The pup begins to think you are his servant. He will not learn the difference between good and bad behavior. If you want to cuddle and pet your pup, first give him a command, such as "Sit." Then your play session with lots of petting is a reward for his obeying a command.
No free-choice feeding	If a pup is fed reliably, same place, same time, same good food every day, he learns that people control the food bowl. Withholding food is not proper, but showing him how reliable you are in the food department builds his confidence in you and gives you opportunities for more behavior training. Have your pup "sit" before you give him food.

What you both should know:

Relax
Enjoy!

The dog is *not* a democratic animal.

It is generally thought that the domestic dog is a direct descendant of the wolf. The wolf is very much a pack animal; that is to say, it recognizes a heirarchy or pecking order of individuals within the pack and the Number One male is the pack leader. It is possible that innate recognition of status within the pack was the behavioral trait which made it possible for man to fit a small wolf into the human family structure. A wolf cub, recognizing authority and rank by nature, was ideally suited to adaptation into the human family. That very basic part of the innate behavior of the wolf still exists today in its descendants, the domestic dog.

If you allow your pup an equal say in his activities, he will interpret that as an offer of pack leadership. He will begin to guide your activities to coincide with his benefits. He'll determine such things as where he wants to sleep, how often he wants to be let in and out of the house, and how much attention he gets. A dog with a more aggressive personality may even go to the extent of not letting you touch his food pan and of growling or snapping if you try to make him do something he doesn't want to do.

An extremely important and necessary factor in raising a puppy is to establish yourself as the pack leader. This involves a conscious effort on your part. It's very easy to let these three months slide by and to think that *your* puppy doesn't need training because he's such a good dog. But in a few months you'll regret that decision. The sweet puppy who never needed puppy training because he never did anything wrong begins to exercise his mature personality. He's not mean, but suddenly he's a lively handful who isn't paying any attention to you because the pattern of communication wasn't established as a puppy. This applies to the toy breeds as well as the large breeds. Three to six months is a good age to reinforce your image as pack leader because the pup still likes to be close to you, it's easy to get his attention and he's easy to discipline.

THE PACK LEADER

Anyone who has been involved in maintaining a group of dogs together in a common environment will know they establish a heirarchy or social order that has a pack leader. Because your dog is a dog he is very aware of social order and will find his position sooner or later. In the family situation many people automatically assume they are the pack leader on the rather uncertain premise of human supremacy over animals. But are you *really* the pack leader and does your dog know it? Many dog behavior problems can occur if you're not the pack leader.

Dogs can experience emotional reactions. They experience frustration when they don't know who is in control of their territory and when they don't know which of their actions are acceptable and which are not. Depending on the dog's personality, this uncertainty might manifest itself in the dog's taking over as pack leader to the point of growling and snapping or of urinating and defecating in the house (after he has been well house-trained). Frustration may also appear as destructive behavior such as ripping furniture, excessive digging in the yard or incessant barking.

We feel it is vitally important for people to understand the pack-leader concept. Establishing the rules of the game can be done easily during puppyhood. It results in a dog who fits into the lifestyle of your home. If minor behavior problems subsequently arise, they are relatively easy to deal with if you and the dog have developed a mutual respect.

The role of leader is abdicated by many people because they see it as the lion-tamer-with-a-whip concept or as a dictator complex with no pleasant communication allowed. This is not the case at all. In a good dog-person relationship (with you as the pack leader), mutual respect is absolutely necessary. The person must respect the dog and must understand the physical and social needs unique to being a canid. On the other hand, the dog must respect you, and he will, if he is treated with consistency and if he knows the rules that you have established are for the mutual benefit of man and dog. Dogs need guidelines and need to know the limits.

How Do You Become the Pack Leader?

It isn't a short-term battle of wills in which you are the victor and the puppy is vanquished. It is built on daily routine. Being the pack leader doesn't mean you must be big and aggressive. A small woman can be pack leader. It's an attitude—an air of authority. It's the basis for the mutual respect that is so important for building a bridge of communication between the two of you.

Many pack-leader activities are a part of the puppy training routine (which is discussed in detail in Chapter 12). "Sit" is the most important command your pup can learn because it is so easy to use as a reminder that you're in charge of things. Tell the pup to "Sit" before you feed him, before you play with him, before you let him go outside. This shows the pup that he must respond to you before he indulges in pleasure for himself and keeps him from becoming a spoiled brat.

As you're teaching him the sit, praise him with a pat on the chest, which is in itself a means of impressing your leadership position on the puppy. Leaning over is canine language for dominance. (In fact, if you have an especially sensitive or shy puppy, you may want to avoid leaning over the pup because it may intimidate him.)

Another good pack-leader exercise involves combining the "Come" with taking the pup on a walk without a leash. For this, you should take the puppy to an area that's uncrowded, preferably with no people at all. Most three-month old pups won't want to get too far away from you, which is another reason this is a good age. Go for a walk together and when the pup gets about twenty-five feet away, get his attention by calling his name and clapping your hands. When he looks at you, kneel down and call him to you. Give him lots of praise when he gets to you and continue your walk, repeating this another three or four times. If you have an independent puppy who ignores you, try running away from him. Many pups can't resist that and will follow. If you have a *very* independent puppy, begin calling him when he's just ten feet away and give him a very small piece of cheese or some other good treat as soon as he gets to you. This exercise reminds the puppy that you're always there and that you're the leader who must be reported to every so often.

You'll be accepted as pack leader by your dog when you're consistent and fair in your demands. For example, if you let the pup jump up on you one day and then the next day you kick or slap him for doing the same thing, the pup will be confused and will wonder when he can do something and when not.

The aspiring pack leader doesn't permit the puppy to growl or snap at him. A severe scruff shaking is necessary when this happens, followed by no attention from you for ten to fifteen minutes. A growl or a snap is not unusual behavior for many pups. It's a natural way for them to show irritation. Usually one or two corrections are all that's necessary to eliminate that behavior. However, if the pup is not corrected, you're asking for big trouble later. Give some thought as to what stimulus provoked the growl or the snap. If the pup has been treated unnecessarily roughly, it's up to you to change the situation.

Walking with a pup helps to put you in the place of pack leader. Periodically stop and call him to you.

How Does a Dog Become the Pack Leader?

Very easily. He's either ignored most of the time or overindulged and smothered with attention. He isn't trained. He isn't taught the difference between good and bad and so he establishes his own criteria with himself as the center of attention. As a result he may become not very pleasant for you or your friends and neighbors to live with. It's supposed to be the other way around—the dog is living in *your* world. Someone has to call the shots and both you and your dog will be happier if it's you.

CONCLUSION

Guide the puppy to behave the way you want him to from the time you bring him home. Be patient. Behavior development takes time. If you're relaxed and don't turn every act of your puppy's into a major battle, you'll find that having a puppy in the house is one of the most delightful experiences you've ever had and that having a mature dog in the house who respects you is deeply rewarding.

CHAPTER 11
THE IMPORTANCE OF PERSONALITY

"Accept your puppy as he is; then mold the kind of dog you want."

Sometimes it's very difficult to see your pup as he really is, rather than as you want him to be. The exuberant, forceful person cannot really believe his pup might be a little short of confidence and need morale-boosting. The quiet person cannot really believe his pup is leader-oriented and must have a firm hand and firm voice. Surely, this assertive little puppy will become sweet and gentle any day now—wishing will make it so. The fact is, you must accept the pup the way he is and then proceed to mold the kind of adult dog you want.

INDIVIDUAL CHARACTERISTICS

The pup's individual genetic qualities determine such factors as the degree of shyness or aggressiveness and other traits such as curiosity and excitability. These traits are found in all breeds, purebred and mongrel alike, and are components in a dog's personality. What is the basic temperament of your puppy? Is he dependent, independent, leader-oriented, aggressive, eager to please, shy, or too easily excited? As the pack leader you will continue to develop a communication with your pup by training him. This needs to be done according to the pup's personality, however, or the training can do more harm than good at this age.

The Dependent Puppy

This pup is usually found in the toy breeds. He looks to his owner for approval for all of his actions and tends to be emotional.

This pup wants constantly to stay very close to his owner and does a minimum of investigating. It's very easy to get in the habit of carrying this puppy, an activity that should be limited because it will exaggerate the dog's dependency to the extent of making him overly nervous. Gentleness is needed in living with this pup. Keep showing the pup what you expect him to do and he'll soon respond. Don't treat this pup like a baby. That will make him an emotional cripple. Just because he's small and acts very dependent upon you doesn't mean he can't learn good puppy behavior.

The Independent Puppy

A little independence is a good thing. There is nothing wrong with having a puppy who thinks for himself at times, but some pups are more inclined this way than others. The sign of a very independent puppy is to not be able to get his attention to come to you when you are only ten feet away calling him. This pup will ignore your voice and your hand clapping, sniff along and go his own merry way. If this pup isn't given puppy training he will be difficult to train as an adult because his desire to please will by then be focused mostly on himself. This pup takes patience and firmness but generally is easy to train because the dog is calm and not emotional. If it's possible, keep the pup in a dog crate or a room or yard area by himself for at least 30 minutes before the training session. This will help to encourage his attention to you. If at first he seems more interested in everything else

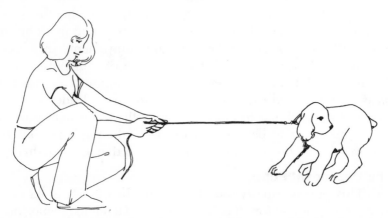

Use a cord to keep the independent puppy under control during the training sessions so that he can never not come when called.

than in you, be patient and show him firmly what you want him to do. Reward him with a pat on the chest or with your voice, "Good dog," or both. You may want to use contingent reward (p. 98) to get his attention. The trick is to keep his attention zeroed in on you. Keep sessions short and be aware that it might take many of them before your pup responds like you want him to.

The Eager-to-Please Puppy

This pup will respond to your voice very quickly and will eagerly come running to you when you call him (from close distances, of course). It will seem as though he learns very quickly because he wants to do what you show him to do. He's so responsive to you that it's easy to mistake this and think that he already knows how to sit or come or stay. However, this pup needs much repetition and will take almost as long to actually learn something as the more independent puppy. This is probably the easiest type to work with. Training sessions can be for longer periods without stressing the puppy. But to begin with, no pup should have more than five minutes at a time. These pups are filled with charm and will readily train you to their desires, so watch for this.

The Shy Puppy

This pup has some distinctive behavior patterns. He may crouch and freeze when you approach him. He may be overly sensitive. He may cringe and stay away if you raise your voice even a little. He may be very fearful in a new place, even though there are no noises or other frightening things. He may not want to approach another person even though the person is quiet and non-frightening. Some pups will roll on their sides or urinate when you show them attention. This is also an indication of excessive submissiveness.

A pup showing signs of submissiveness.

Guide the puppy gently but firmly to do what you want him to do, then follow a couple of minutes of working with a short play period. Improvement will be slow, but it will come. The pup may not want to participate in learning any of the commands such as Sit or Come or Stay, but keep repeating the learning sessions with lots of patience.

You must be the pack leader for this puppy also. If you're not, the pup will take over the job. He can see that he has you trained to let him act the way he wants to. For example, if you feel sorry for this pup when he starts to act shy and frightened and you begin to pet him, you are rewarding his behavior and encouraging him to act that way in the future. Instead, when he begins to act shy, speak to him in a pleasant, firm voice but don't pet him until his behavior is more what you want it to be, even if for only a split second. It is especially important to make the training sessions fun. Keep his mind on you and off himself.

This pup was born with a short supply of confidence and he will need a lot of patience from you. His behavior will gradually improve as your pup gets confidence in himself and in you.

The Dominant Puppy Who Competes for Pack Leadership

The dominant-aggressive pup is a very active one and demands a lot of attention. He's little and cute and it's very easy to give him all the attention he wants. He becomes spoiled because of the overindulgence. Then the aggressive tendency shows up as he grows older and you don't want to cater to him anymore. He will let you know he's unhappy with you.

The competitive puppy might snap at you if you reach down to move his feed pan while he's eating or may snap at you during leash training if he decides he doesn't want to stay at your side. In other words, the pup will try to do things his way and if you permit this you are setting yourself up for serious and difficult to correct behavior as he gets older. Aggressive actions in the puppy cannot be permitted. We can't stress strongly enough the importance of not allowing the aggressive puppy to become the dominant member of the relationship.

When the pup snaps at you it will be a shock and a surprise, but don't retreat because this is what he wants. This rewards his snapping and encourages him to do it again. Use a severe scruff shaking. When this type of puppy needs to be disciplined he shouldn't be slapped or beaten because he might take it as a challenge and fight back.

Puppy training is essential for the leader-oriented pup. It teaches him that he receives a reward for obeying, for submitting to your commands. Teach the pup the Sit command and use it constantly. This keeps reminding the pup that you're the boss.

The Extremely Excitable Puppy

All puppies can become excited easily, but some won't calm down. Some you can hardly touch because they are constantly wiggling. Such a pup will really try your patience. He's difficult to work with because you can't get his attention for more than a few seconds. You may need to start with sessions that are less than a minute long. They can gradually become longer as the pup learns to pay attention. Try not to add to his excitement by any quick motions on your part. Stay calm with as little body movement as possible. Keep repeating the training routine. Don't pet him or tell him he's a good dog until you've finished the training session. Sometimes it helps if the pup is allowed to run off some of his energy in a supervised enclosure before the training lesson begins. Then put the leash on and tell him school is in session.

If over a period of time you've tried the puppy training routine everyday and you see no improvement, there may be a physiological reason for the pup's behavior. In a few cases, some pups are so excitable that you can't hold their attention long enough to even begin training. These are signs of over-excitability, in which case you should get the help of a veterinarian. Certain dogs have a problem similar to hyperactive children and respond to similar treatment. If you think this might be the case, discuss it with your veterinarian.

THE TRAINER'S PERSONALITY

Your personality is also a factor in puppy training. If you are very shy—or quite assertive—this may indeed affect your pup's reactions to you. Be aware of how you are coming across to your pup. If necessary, moderate your approach. Usually, though, a pup will adjust to your individual personality and will want to do things your way as long as you're consistent and he knows what you want him to do. Within the bounds of respecting your pup and not abusing him, your method of dog training should be what seems natural to you. It's up to you to decide if you're being too tough on your pup or too lenient. Be honest with yourself. Open your eyes. Your pup is continually telling you how things really are and what kind of training he needs from you. Puppy training is a one-on-one propositon. Trust your instincts. Listen to your pup; read his body language. He can tell you a lot more than your neighbor can.

As different as breed and genetic characteristics might be in a population of puppies, almost any one of them, if given adequate socialization, can learn to respond to humans in a very satisfactory way.

CHAPTER 12
PUPPY TRAINING

The one most important factor in raising and training a puppy from three to six months is getting the puppy to pay attention to you.

The pack-leader image and your puppy training depend on your being able to get your pup's attention. This is the basis of puppy activity at this age. It is essential to having a well-behaved adult dog.

Puppy training is an exercise for the puppy's brain and his now well-developed central nervous system. The pup is ready for input, a piece at a time, but he's not a computer. It will be several months before he can put all the pieces together.

When it comes to living with you, puppies have to learn everything about how to behave. They may have been born with a strong desire to please, but they still need to learn how to pay attention to you when you speak. They may have been very well-socialized and love you dearly, but they still need to learn they must come to you *every* time you call them even if there's a dead frog that's much more interesting.

Many people say they don't want a "trained" dog. They apparently fear that any type of instruction will destroy the pup's beautiful free spirit. If they only knew how much happier their dog would be with some discipline, they wouldn't be able to get started soon enough. When training is geared to the dog's basic personality it can only increase the pup's feeling of self-confidence, which in turn makes the dog enjoy training even more as he gets older. In other words, he'll be an even happier spirit as well as much more pleasant to have around.

PUPPY TRAINING vs. OBEDIENCE TRAINING

Puppy training is different from obedience training for adult dogs. The main purpose in puppy training is to build a communication system between the two of you. *You are teaching your dog how to learn.* You may think this doesn't seem very important because it doesn't involve a stern attitude with a lot of jerking and punishing. But we promise you that "puppy training" can make a difference in your dog's behavior and his trainability for the rest of his life.

In contrast to the positive approach of puppy training, many obedience classes use a lot of leash jerking and a certain amount of punishment if the dog isn't performing well. There's a fine line between the two attitudes and it's a vitally important difference. With a young puppy, if you're forcing him to perform perfectly and punishing him even mildly if he doesn't, you may be asking for trouble later on. After a puppy is six to eight months old, he can usually begin to handle corrections and accept much more firmness in his training but not at three, four and five months of age.

The puppy's emotional system must be allowed to mature before he can learn to accept negative training. Stress shouldn't be a specific part of puppy training. That comes later when the pup is six to eight months old and ready for more formal training. Of course, it's not possible or necessary to completely avoid stress because there's often a small amount in any of a puppy's activities. However, we want to eliminate stress as a planned part of the actual training.

Attending a training class for puppies can be a good experience if the class is very small in size and if the instructor doesn't use the same methods for both puppies and adult dogs. But a class isn't necessary. Having determined the nature of your puppy's personality you can now go ahead with a simple training program which is tailor-made to get the best from your puppy.

IMPORTANT BASIC INFORMATION
FOR PUPPY TRAINING

The same basic guidelines apply to all pups. Whatever your pup's pedigree and whatever your goals for him, any puppy is still an emotionally immature animal. The only difference in starting hunting or field trial pups, for example, would be the addition of different field activities but the principles are the same.

No two pups are exactly alike and what works for one puppy, for example in teaching the "Sit," isn't necessarily best for another. You must constantly be aware of your pup's personality and of how you can get him to pay attention to you. However, there are some general characteristics of puppy training that are important to working with all puppies. These are basic principles which should be adapted by you as the basis of working with your puppy.

Don't get tough: Emotionally and psychologically, the pup is still extremely sensitive. This means that learning takes place quickly, but also that fears can easily occur and inhibit learning. Pups cannot take pressure or harsh treatment.

Repetition is the key to puppy training. Don't punish the pup if he doesn't do what you want him to. This will defeat the purpose of the training and cause the pup to dislike the entire procedure. Bad behavior during training sessions is more often than not a sign of the pup's lack of confidence or understanding of what you want him to do. Many, many repetitions will be needed.

Keep it simple: A pup learns to do things in a step-by-step manner. For example, in teaching your puppy to stay, you can't expect him to stay put for several minutes at a time while you are off someplace away from him. You must first teach him to stay while you stand toe-to-toe in front of him, then to stay when you're standing a couple of feet out in front of him, then to stay while you walk around him, then to stay while you are standing several feet away and not holding on to the leash. Many pups will take several weeks to progress through these steps, but they are necessary if you want to teach "Stay" effectively.

If you tell a pup to do something before you've properly trained him to do it and then you scold him for not doing it, you're asking for trouble. The pup will lose his confidence and will learn not to try. The same pup given a simple step-by-step training approach will become a dog who not only is eager to learn but is ready for more complicated training as he gets older.

Be brief: Puppies have a very short attention span. A pup learns only while he's paying attention to you, so it doesn't accomplish anything to keep on training when the pup is mentally tired even though physically he's still very lively. Five minutes at a time is long enough. With many puppies, two minutes is long enough to begin with, gradually moving up to five mintues.

Build confidence: Your pup needs confidence-building as well as discipline and he'll constantly be telling you by his body language which one he needs more at any particular time. If your pup is out of control and not paying any attention to you, he may need a vigorous scruff shaking to settle him down. If your pup is too quiet and has a hang-dog look, he needs more confidence building. Relax while you're with the puppy, smile, speak in a pleasant voice, play running games with him. In puppy training, building confidence means knowing what you expect from your pup. Concentrate on what you're doing. Think positive. Picture the proper procedure in your mind and have an attitude of enthusiasm and success.

It's important at this age for the pup to feel he's a valuable individual. Do everything you can to have your training sessions in a relatively quiet place. Because he's so playful, the pup is easily distracted by other people and activities. If he's constantly being bombarded by other sights and sounds, it will be difficult for him to get the message from you that you enjoy being with him and think he's wonderful.

Use words: Don't expect your pup to be a mind reader. The only way he'll learn to associate the command with the action is if you use the word every time you guide him into doing what you want. A puppy can learn a very large vocabulary with such words as "Outdoors," "Bedtime," "Go for a walk," as well as the common commands.

Reward your pup: To teach your pup anything, you must first have his attention and then you must reward him as soon as he has done what you ask. The reward can take three forms—a tidbit, a pat or your voice.

We consider the use of tidbits (contingent reward) a highly successful means of puppy training. By guiding the pup's behavior with the use of tidbits, you can avoid pushing and pulling with your hands and all of the jerking and pulling on the leash. We especially like to use cheese in very small chunks. It's not messy, requires no chewing and can be used even after it dries out.

A puppy learns much more quickly when he performs the activity himself rather than being pushed or pulled into doing it. Then, as he begins to understand what you mean by "Sit" or "Come" or whatever, you can use your hand or leash to perfect the performance, thereby keeping handling at a minimum.

Timing is of the utmost importance when using contingent reward in puppy training. Obviously, your puppy isn't going to know what you mean by the different commands when you first begin to train him, and the only way he'll learn that he's doing the right thing is if he receives a reward at the moment he does it. An example is using contingent reward to teach the Sit. If you have a very antsy puppy who much prefers bouncing and absolutely hates sitting, you may have to begin by rewarding a bending of the hind legs. If you were to wait until the pup sits all the way down with his bottom on the floor, you would never get the job done. After a few rewards for partial sitting, the puppy will suddenly sit all the way—at which time you'll not only reward him but tell him how marvelous he is.

Another example of contingent reward is with the heeling exercise (or walking alongside, a more appropriate term for puppies). This is the most difficult thing for most puppies to learn. Too often, it involves excessive jerking on the leash. The more a puppy is being pulled, the more he resists and pulls in the opposite direction. Consequently, heeling is very difficult for puppies to learn. Their natural tendency is to run off and sniff around. We have found that using cheese tidbits is very effective in overcoming the problems of teaching a puppy to walk beside us. It works even better off-leash *(but only for a minute at a time)*. As you begin walking, the instant the pup begins to look away from you, get his attention with your voice and give him a tidbit. This will keep him at your side for another few steps. Repeat this a few times during each session, reversing your direction and taking some turns. Then stop while you're both still performing well and give the pup lots of praise with your voice and some pats as well.

After the pup has a good idea of what you want him to do, begin to ease off using tidbits every time. Give him one every other time for awhile, then every third time until finally you cease except for one at the end of the training session.

Don't let yourself use tidbits as a bribe. It's very easy to fall into the trap of thinking that if you give a pup a treat he'll be good. But what does this look like from the dog's viewpoint? It looks like you are treating him as top dog and whatever he wants to do is okay with you. So only use tidbits when you're teaching a specific thing and then only long enough to be sure he has learned it and associates the act with the word for it. Then ease off to the point of stopping the use.

Don't expect overnight results: Try to stay relaxed as you work with the pup. Puppies learn in spurts and starts. One day he may know absolutely everything and perform to perfection. The next day it's as though he never had a moment's training. Too many trainers make the mistake of thinking that if their puppy does it right once or twice he knows it forever—but it really takes hundreds of repetitions for a puppy to learn something. He may go through several periods of confusion in the process. You may think he's mad at you or trying to spite you. But in reality, he's probably trying to tell you that he's confused for some reason. This is often caused by some factor that you're not aware of. You've done something a little differently or the environment has changed in some way and his confidence has been shaken. Try to determine what the cause of the change in behavior might be and then continue your training program. It will all iron out with time and effort.

At first the routine of teaching the puppy to do what you want will take special thought on your part, but after a while it will become automatic and you'll be teaching without realizing it. A puppy or a dog needs *at least* one month of consistent daily repetition before any action becomes a part of his routine. A good rule of thumb is to train the pup consistently for one month, then continue for one month longer than you think is necessary. Then you can expect the pup to know what you're talking about, but you must continue daily use of the commands, using an occasional reminder when the pup is having an "off" day.

Be consistent: There is a wide range of individual approaches to working with a puppy. Each person will be guiding his own puppy to live in harmony with the lifestyle of that particular home. Just as with raising children, there are many different learning environments that can, each one, be successful. The key to success is to be consistent in your demands and your discipline.

Puppies need feedback: A pup learns by getting feedback from his owner. Praise your pup so he'll know when he's done something right. Otherwise he'll never learn what it is you want him to do. Then he'll get confused because you keep nagging him and hollering at him and he doesn't know why. He'll turn into a hyperactive nervous wreck. So let him know when he's done a good job.

Hands off: Keep your hands off the pup as much as possible except to pat in praise. It may be necessary once in awhile to manipulate the pup with your hands, but this should be the exception—it's much too easy to get into the habit of constantly grabbing, pushing and pulling. A puppy isn't learning unless he's actually doing the action himself. This is why it's so important to guide the pup into doing what you want. The actions (sit, heel, come) that the pup repeats under his own power quickly become a part of his conditioning and he'll begin to repeat them willingly. Using a tidbit as a reward is effective because it lets you guide the puppy's actions to do what you want and the immediate reward sets it in his brain.

If you take all the previous points into consideration, you are automatically teaching your pup to pay attention. By adhering to his physical and psychological needs, you'll find that he'll respond to you and you'll be well on your way to building a good puppy-person relationship.

THE MECHANICS OF PUPPY TRAINING

Equipment

The buckle-type collar is definitely the best kind to use for puppies. If you must use a chain collar, be sure to fasten the leash to the dead ring. Don't put the leash on the ring that pulls up and chokes the pup. Choke training is for older dogs and is not a good training procedure for pups. Be sure the collar is comfortable, neither too long nor too short. You may need several sizes as the pup grows.

The leash should be about six feet long and may be made of anything except chain. Leather is most preferable; it's so easy to work with and comfortable in your hand. A canvas leash is also very good, and a piece of soft rope will get the job done.

What Time of Day is Best?

Experts believe that regularly scheduled, short training periods give the best results. However, this isn't always possible in the average household and doesn't mean you can't adequately train your puppy by using unscheduled sessions.

Puppy training fits into your lifestyle whatever it may be. Don't say you don't have time to train your pup. Wherever and whenever you have a few minutes, go through the basic commands. If supper isn't quite ready, take five minutes to do some Sits and Stays. Whenever you go in or out a door or gate, tell the pup to "Stay." Use your foot to gently guide the pup at first. Point your finger at him when you say "Stay." He'll quickly learn not to go in or out until you say, "Okay."

Times that aren't good for training are just after the pup has eaten and at the end of a vigorous play period. Before each of these times, however, is an excellent time for a few minutes of training.

Teaching the Sit

The quickest way to teach the Sit is to hold a tidbit above the pup's head. When the pup leans back and sits, praise him with the tidbit. Say "Sit" each time. After a good many repetitions, the puppy will begin to associate the word with the action.

Another way to teach the Sit is to put your hand across the back of the pup's hind legs. Say "Sit" at the same time that you quickly push his knees in and gently pull up on the leash. Praise him. This is good for pups who react to being touched on their bodies. A technique that also works well is to put your hand on the pup's side just in front of his hind leg, with your thumb on his back. Press down at the same time you pull up gently on the leash.

Teaching the Sit-Stay

Don't begin working on the stay until the puppy is sitting readily and don't expect a puppy to stay for longer than a few seconds. Work up to a minute by six months of age. If you get in a hurry and expect the pup to stay too long too soon, he'll break his stay and you'll be teaching him that it's okay not to wait for you to excuse him from your command.

Teach the Sit-Stay in a step-by-step manner. Don't progress to the next step until your pup is steady at the previous one. Begin by having the pup sit at your side. Move your feet just a quarter of

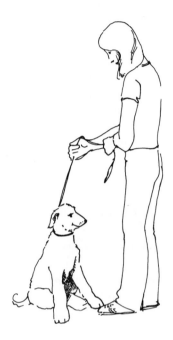

a turn after saying "Stay." (Don't move away from the pup. Stand in place and just move your body and foot position.) Move back immediately and praise the pup. When he has learned to tolerate your brief movement without trying to stand up, add another quarter turn and stand toe-to-toe in front of the pup. Keep the leash straight up over his head. When the pup breaks his stay, you can keep him from moving out of position. Give a quick upward tug on the leash, repeat the stay command and start over. Eventually, your pup will learn to stay as you walk in a circle around him. Your pup should perform well at each successive manuever. You can't skip stages. Don't do more than three or four Stays in succession with a puppy.

Teaching the Come

Use body language as well as words. For example, make a clapping motion with your hands. Kneel down on the pup's level. Be sure the pup is close to you, looking at you, before you tell him to come. Distance comes later—much later. Begin using "Come" from seven weeks on. The young puppy loves to come running and lick you in the face. You're his whole world. Take advantage of this. Give him lots of "Comes" in the house whenever you have the opportunity. Most of the "Comes" with young puppies will be off leash.

Both the shy and the independent puppy may resist coming to you. There are a couple of things you can do to overcome this problem. Get the pup excited while standing right in front of him, then turn and run away, encouraging him to follow. After eight to ten feet, give lots of happy praise. If this doesn't work, run backwards facing the pup and encourage him to follow you. This is also an excellent way of conditioning the pup to come to you when you're outdoors. Turning and running the opposite direction is a signal for him to come looking for you before you disappear.

If you have an excitable pup who gets very involved in sniffing, you may find that using a tidbit reward as soon as the pup gets to you is very effective. You must begin the "Come" at very short distances, maybe even three to four feet. Begin as close as necessary to get the pup's attention and to achieve success.

Use visual cues like clapping your hands as well as calling the pup's name.

Teaching Heeling

It isn't natural for a pup to walk slowly, so move at a pace that will keep him trotting at your side. When his attention wanders, pat your left leg; talk to him; do a quick reverse. When he's back at your side, tell him how good he is. Keep his attention by keeping him jogging and by talking to him and by giving him tidbits. If your pup is constantly pulling your arm off, something is wrong with the way you're doing things. The pup is ignoring you. If necessary, stop and give him a scruff-shaking. Then continue.

Use the leash to keep the pup under control and to correct any movement immediately.

Keep the pup's attention on you. Use your voice. Pat your leg.

Get your pup's attention the moment he becomes distracted.

After a few sessions of encouraging your puppy to stay close to your side while walking with you, begin to exert a little more formal control. Give the pup a couple of small tugs on his collar immediately after you say "Heel" at the same time you begin walking forward. This little tug with the leash (not a jerk that spins the puppy off his feet) acts as a cue and tells the pup, "Now we're ready to begin walking."

Work on heeling for just a minute or two at a time. As you and the puppy begin to work well together you can gradually extend the length of time. If on any one day you see you're losing the pup's attention and you can't seem to work together, stop training. The next session will be better. Dogs and people can both have "off" days.

A SUMMARY OF THE BASIC PRINCIPLES OF PUPPY TRAINING

1. Get your pup's attention:

   How? a. Be the Boss.
           b. Talk to your pup.
           c. Concentrate on what you're doing.
           d. Keep training sessions short.

2. Remember the "opposing force" reflex:

   Every time you *pull*, your pup will automatically *resist* with opposite force.
   Every time you *push*, your pup will automatically *resist* with opposite force.

   This is why guiding your pup must be done quickly and firmly. If you are too slow and heavy-handed, your pup is using his energy in opposing you rather than in learning what you're trying to teach. If your guiding actions are quick, your dog finds himself doing what you want and he is happy.

3. Praise your puppy:

   Your pup wants to please you, but you must show him what makes you happy. For example, if lying quietly at your feet makes you happy, occasionally praise your pup when he is doing this. If walking at your side without jerking and pulling makes you happy, praise him whenever he does this. When he doesn't, use your voice and your body movements to attract his attention.

Praise is a much more powerful teaching tool than spanking, pushing, pulling and shouting, but it must be administered with concentration and good timing on your part to be effective.

4. Teach your pup step-by-step:

Your pup learns best if what he is learning is divided into steps. Teach your pup as if you are building with blocks. Each activity is a combination of blocks added one at a time until the finished product has been accomplished.

For example: in teaching the sit-stay, be certain your pup is steady at each step of the way. Don't walk round your pup in a circle until he's steady when you stand in front of him. Don't stand six feet in front of him until he's steady when you walk in a close circle. Test him at each step by using distractions such as different sounds and different body movements.

5. Enjoy. Training should be a pleasant experience—for both you and your pup:

A pleasant experience for you is having a happy pup who pays attention.

A pleasant experience for your pup is having a master who demands attention and who rewards with praise for a job well done.

CHAPTER 13
THE SECOND SIX MONTHS

"Now your pup is sexually mature, but he is still a puppy and he still needs firm guidance."

There comes a day when you wonder what's wrong. Your pup won't pay attention to you. In fact, he seems to be going out of his way to oppose you. Well, nothing's wrong—it's just one of the difficult times a dog goes through (difficult for you but not for him). At six or seven months of age and again around twelve months your dog will challenge your leadership. This is a very normal dog thing for your pup to do so don't get upset. Tell the pup that you know what he's doing, and that you're still the boss.

You'll probably have to specifically show him that you're the boss by calling his bluff. When he begins ignoring your commands by sniffing the ground or scratching an imaginary itch or just playing deaf, MOVE QUICKLY! Give the pup a scruff shake or a collar correction. Sometimes just a voice correction will shape him up. It depends on your pup's personality. But whatever you do, *don't* stand around waiting for him to get in the mood. Don't sweet-talk him or coax him, because what would this tell the pup? He's testing you to see if you're really the pack leader. And you're showing him that you're not, that you will wait for him, that he can "Sit" or "Come" or "Heel" on his terms whenever he's ready and interested. This makes him the pack leader and it means that he's training you! So get busy with that quick correction. We keep telling you that being the pack leader is based on your attitude and on day-to-day activities. This is another example of what we mean.

PERSONALITY

Your pup's personality will continue to change during the next few months. Some behavior traits don't become strongly developed until the dog is a year old or more. Traits such as stubborness and extreme independence were undoubtedly hinted at during puppyhood but were very easy to ignore because "he's only a puppy," or because it hadn't become a problem yet. If you have trained you puppy in accordance with his personality type, you have likely nipped many problems before they have become deeply entrenched, but, as the dog matures, you must continue to assert your role of leadership.

Some behavior traits aren't very noticeable until the dog reaches sexual maturity, and then they can become obvious problems requiring attention. Roaming and over-protectiveness are some examples of these. Some dogs have a genetic disposition toward aggression or protectiveness, and sexual maturity accentuates it. Castration will curb the roaming behavior and might affect aggression toward other male dogs but most probably won't affect aggression toward people.

Other behavior problems such as barking or a lapse in housetraining can be caused by stress or a change in the daily home routine. Such stresses might include a stay in a boarding kennel or a schedule change by a member of the family who had previously been at home and then went back to school or work.

It is because some behavior traits don't show up until after puppyhood (for whatever reason) that we have emphasized the importance of puppy training. If you wait until your pup becomes too independent or territorially protective, for example, before you begin to try to have some control over your dog, then you have a long hard job ahead of you. Puppy training is a good way to avoid some of the problems before they become a habit with the dog.

TERRITORIALITY

Almost all dogs have a sense of territory. Unless a dog has been totally forbidden to do so, he will automatically announce the arrival of someone at the door or on the property. Some dogs have stronger than average senses of territory and enlarge their area to include the route of their regular walks through the neighborhood. An aggressive male dog could become a problem because of trying to fight other males who are intruding on his street or his sidewalk. The degree of a dog's protective actions depends partly on his breed characteristics and his individual personality. It can range from barking for a period of time to growling to aggressively approaching the stranger.

The degree of the dog's protective actions is based on the relationship you have established with him as a puppy. If you have been wishy-washy and have let the pup have his own way it will begin to show at this age. The pup will begin to put himself in the role of pack leader. This means that if he has tendencies toward over-protectiveness he will begin to become overly aggressive and may snap if someone comes near his food bowl, or growl at your friends. Some people think they want a guard dog and thus should allow their puppies to behave this way. This is not correct, however. A dog who is not controllable is dangerous to have around. It isn't necessary to encourage aggressive actions in order to have a dog who barks aggressively and warns you of strangers. Most dogs will automatically do this. If you want a guard dog, have a reputable trainer work with you and your dog and remember that the key word is "control."

SEXUAL MATURITY

The Female

The indication that the female has reached sexual maturity is the occurrence of the onset of estrus, commonly called the heat period. There is a lot of variation within breeds as well as among breeds and even in the cycle of one bitch from one heat to the next. However, there are some generalizations that can be used as a valid basis for discussion. These are reported in an autotutorial unit by Kerry Kettring, DVM, Ohio State University.

With intense domestication of the dog the seasonal breeding characteristics have generally been lost. In other words, dogs can come into heat throughout the year, not just in the spring or fall. Basenjis are the main exception to this, still demonstrating only one estrus per year.

Traditional thought held that estrus occurred every six months, with some of the larger breeds having intervals of about nine months. However, recent studies have shown that the dog's size is not specifically related to the length of the period between heats. The Cairn Terrier, Pekingese, Labrador and Rhodesian Ridgeback each has a breed average of an interval of twenty-nine weeks; these breeds range in size from ten to seventy pounds. Other averages range from twenty-six weeks for the German Shepherd to thirty-six weeks for the Collie. It must always be remembered that there are variations within each breed also.

There is an apparent correlation between breed size and the onset of the first estrus. It generally occurs at six to eight months for less than thirty pounds, eight to ten months for thirty to sixty pounds and ten to fifteen months for breeds greater than sixty pounds.

The heat period begins with a distinct turgid swelling of the vulva and a bright red discharge. This usually lasts seven to nine days (proestrus). The estrus stage is the second week, lasting from seven to eight days, when the vulva is flaccid and swollen with a straw-colored discharge (or possibly no discharge). It is during this stage that a bitch can be bred. The last stage of the heat period is metestrus. It lasts two to three days and the discharge is usually chocolate or clear in color.

Most bitches follow a general pattern of behavior. The bitch is attractive to the male beginning with the proestrus stage but usually will not permit a breeding attempt until she is in the estrus stage. Many experienced male dogs won't even make a serious attempt during the proestrus stage, with the exception of an aggressive or inexperienced male. On entering estrus the bitch becomes playful and will usually allow a breeding to take place as well as permit other females to mount her. She will hold her tail up and to the side, often beginning this action a couple of days before she is actually in estrus. A bitch who is extremely nervous or aggressive may never allow a male to mount her. Some bitches act quite silly just before and during the heat period and not much training can be accomplished during estrus. Their concentration is definitely elsewhere. Many bitches are very active during the estrus stage, probably as a result of the secretion of estrogen.

The Male

At some time during the last half of the first year, a male will begin to lift his leg to urinate. This is usually viewed as a mark of the sexually maturing male. This can begin at anywhere from five to twelve months, or even later. Sexual maturity often brings on an increased attitude of protectiveness and an intense interest in other dogs. As we have already stated, you may have to take specific steps to reinforce your position as pack leader.

After the male reaches the age where he is leg-lifting, he might begin to do it to excess. Leg-lifting is the manner in which a male marks his territory. Many people think they must allow their dog to stop at every blade of grass if that is what the dog wants. (Who's the pack leader?) Excessive leg-lifting is often a demonstration that the dog has a strong tendency toward being the pack leader and this is one way of telling you he's taking over the job. In small breeds, this might occur in the house. Leg-lifting to such an excess isn't necessary. It isn't pleasant to take a dog for a walk if he's constantly stopping to lift his leg. Therefore, during your walk, have a couple of stops where he can lift his leg several times. Then continue the walk at a brisk pace on your terms. The routine can be adjusted to fit the involved individuals as long as the dog gets his bladder empty and as long as you remain the pack leader.

SPAY AND NEUTER

One of the ways in which dogs can be helped to adjust to an urban or suburban environment is to spay or neuter them. This is not mistreating the dog or depriving him of natural feelings that are his "right." If the hormones don't send the message to the brain the dog doesn't know what he's missing. In fact, it makes his life more pleasant because it removes some of the behavior traits with which people find it difficult to live.

The Spay or Ovariohysterectomy

The behavior of the bitch remains normal after the spay operation because this is the natural condition of the female between heat periods. A common myth about spaying is that the bitch becomes fat and lazy. If these should occur it's a result of overfeeding and underexercising. There is also a common belief that a female should have one heat period before being spayed but there is no definite evidence such a delay has any effect on the bitch's future behavior. Therefore, if you would like to avoid the problem of confining the bitch while she's in heat, it would be best to try to time the spay operation shortly before her first heat period. If she won't be spayed until after her heat period it's a good idea to wait for about two months because it takes this long for the progesterone level to decline completely. If progestin secretion is suddenly stopped, nervousness or irritability may occur for a time. This can be offset, however, by having your veterinarian administer a long-acting progestin.

Neutering or Castration

Neutering does not change the dog's masculine appearance because he will still acquire his secondary sex characteristics. A study conducted by Dr. Benjamin Hart and reported in his book, *Canine Behavior,* indicates that castration doesn't affect hunting ability or watchdog behavior. There are individual differences in how castration affects other behaviors. Some differences are probably a result of the environment but many are due to breed and genetics. Roaming showed the greatest degree of change with over 90 percent of the dogs having either a rapid or gradual decline. This is probably a result of the lessening in sexual drive. Fighting with other male dogs showed 40 percent to have a rapid decline and 22 percent a gradual decline. About 50 percent showed a decline in urine marking in the house. The act of mounting dropped rapidly in about one-third of the dogs studied and gradually declined in another one-third. Much of this decline was in mounting people so castration appears to be a good way to reduce this problem.

There doesn't appear to be any proven difference in effect from castration before puberty or in the adult dog. And as is true with the female spay operation, there is no basis for the idea that castrated dogs become fat and lazy. Some trainers have noted that early neutering of shy males helps to improve their excessive shyness.

TRAINING

From six to twelve months is a good time to begin some of the specific formal training that is involved in field trialing, obedience trials and showing. During these months the maturing dog can't yet be expected to put it all together and come up with a mature performance because obviously that takes more experience and concentration than he has acquired so far. But if he is to be expected to perform well and fit into his role in life, whether as a champion or a family companion, it is important that formal training be continued throughout these six months. This is an excellent way to continue a close relationship with the dog and to maintain your position as pack leader. It doesn't matter what kind of training you want to do with your dog. Maybe it's entertaining stunts such as described in the book, *Dog Tricks: Teaching Your Dog to Be Useful,* by Haggerty and Benjamin. What is important is you and your dog working together on a one-to-one basis.

Most dogs are now ready for a more intense training schedule and can be expected to take corrections and to attain a high standard in performing their tasks correctly. However, it must be remembered that they still learn complicated activities best if the task is divided into small units. You must also continue to let the dog know when he's performed correctly and when he has goofed.

As your pup continues to grow and change in size as well as behavior, adjust your own attitudes toward him accordingly. Always try to step back and look at the two of you objectively. Picture your last training session as though it were a movie you're watching. Then analyze it. What kind of signals is your dog sending? Is he cowering or dragging you at the end of the leash or simply ignoring you? What signals are you giving your dog? Are you seldom doing anything the same way twice or being terribly stern and forbidding? What can you do about it? Do you need to spend more time with your dog, be more consistent in your training, or maybe ease up a bit? It's perfectly permissible to be pleasant and even smile while training your dog. If your pup is paying attention to you and accepts your guiding his activities and your corrections when he gets a little silly or assertive, then you know you're on the right path.

The dog is now ready to learn more formal discipline that requires a greater degree of self control.

AFTERWORD

You've brought your puppy a long way and have developed a good communication system. Now you can look forward to a long and satisfying relationship which sometimes will take more effort than you care to spend and at other times will have more rewards than you had dared to hope for.

If you have helped your puppy to become a good family member, then you have in a small but nonetheless significant way contributed to helping the dog become a better and consequently more acceptable part of modern society. In this event we would like to congratulate and thank you for joining the ranks of dog lovers in our combined effort to foster good interaction between man and dog, thereby enriching all our lives. If we had a much higher proportion of well-cared for, well-behaved animals and less of the wandering freak hounds, the dog's image with the growing army of the urban and rural disgruntled might not be so bad.

ABOUT THE AUTHORS

Clarice Rutherford's current position is coordinator for the Office of Program Ethics and Federal Compliance Committees at Colorado State University, Fort Collins, Colorado. She has received degrees in Animal Sciences and English. Her life-long fascination with dogs began with the cow dogs on her grandparents' Pennsylvania Dairy Farm and continued with smooth fox terrier mix dogs while growing up in Cleveland and Phoenix. She and her husband have lived with various breeds since then. In addition, her work with 4-H dog obedience introduced her to a wide range of dog personalities.

The Rutherfords have concentrated on Labradors for the past 15 years. Clarice has handled her Labs to a breed championship, obedience titles, and is active in field trialing. She says that the longer she works with dogs the more respect she has for their individual personalities and the more despair she feels for the frustrations dogs must have when their efforts to communicate their needs to people fail. She doubts that any other domestic animal is more taken for granted, and firmly believes that people must be educated to look at the dog with a newly objective point of view. Her activities in CARE (Companion Animal Research and Education) are an attempt to help the urban dweller better understand his dog.

Clarice believes that the days are gone forever when a puppy can be brought home and allowed to just "grow up" with no bother or training. This may have been possible in the past when a family member was at home throughout the day and when the dog had other dog friends in the neighborhood and dogs and people grew up together. Unfortunately, if more people don't begin to understand the needs of the young dog, then we're heading for the day when the dog will not be allowed in our

people-crowded communities. Clarice doesn't want to think of a
world without dogs. She believes that most dog behavior problems can be avoided or nipped in the beginning if a pup is given
attention and puppy training during the first six months, followed by additional training the second six months. To know
this, and then to see maladjusted dogs who can't live with people
because their owners haven't known how to live with a puppy is
heartbreaking. This book is her attempt to help the puppy and
his family live happily together.

David Neil has been Director of Animal Care at Colorado
State University since 1976. Prior to that he held a variety of
positions with the Canadian federal government in Ottawa and
was Chief of the Animal Resources Division of the Health Protection Branch, Health and Welfare Canada immediately before
moving to Colorado.

Dr. Neil received his veterinary degree from the University of
Liverpool in the United Kingdom in 1959 and was in mixed
private practice in Wales and then England for three years. During that time he came to rely heavily on the almost uncanny
ability of the working sheep dogs, particularly where the treatment of large flocks was involved.

In 1962 he was commissioned in the Royal Army Veterinary
Corps, where he first encountered the training of war dogs. The
majority of the dogs were trained for guard duty accompanied by
a handler at military installation, but specialist dogs of other
types were also trained by the Corps for such activities as ambush
detection, detection of anti-personnel mines and hidden wea-
pons, as messenger dogs, and casualty detecting dogs. Subsequently, Neil became involved in researching methods of
protecting these specialist animals from chemical warfare when
in combat zones. This work coincided with an extensive training
period in the care and use of experimental animals in research,
and ultimately led to a career as a laboratory animal veterinarian.
This career raised many ethical questions in David Neil's mind,
and brought him face to face with the issues of man's use of, and
interaction with, domestic animals. He often has said that this
preoccupation conveniently fills the other six hours in his thirty
hour days!

He is very active in the humane movement and was president
of the Larimer County Humane Society from 1978 to 1981. He is
involved in teaching animal control officers from all over the
United States in courses under the auspices of the Humane

Society of the United States and the American Humane Association. Neil is a founding member of CARE (Companion Animal Research and Education) formerly The Center for Research into Canine-Human Interaction, at Colorado State University.

Much has been learned by scientists about canine behavior in the last 30 years. It is unfortunate that in the past so little of this information has been used to facilitate a better understanding of the problems of the dog in contemporary society. This is now changing, and David Neil hopes that the future activities of the experts across the nation, and in CARE, will serve to promote a mutually beneficial relationship between man and dog.

Want to know more about your dog?

The following titles may be ordered direct, or purchased at your local bookstore or pet supply shop.

YES! Please send me:

Qty.

_____ **Positively Obedient, Good Manners for the Family Dog.**
Barbara Handler. $8.95

_____ **Best Foot Forward - Complete Guide to Obedience Handling.**
Barbara Handler. $5.95

_____ **Owner's Guide to Better Behavior in Dogs & Cats.**
William Campbell. $12.95

_____ **Canine Reproduction - A Breeder's Guide.**
Phyllis A. Holst, DVM. $17.95

_____ **Scent - Training to Track, Search, & Rescue.**
Pearsall & Verbruggen. $15.95

_____ **Canine Hip Dysplasa and Other Orthopedic Diseases.**
Fred L. Lanting. $14.95

_____ **Running With Man's Best Friend.**
Davia Anne Gallup. $7.95

Please add $2.00 shipping for 1st book, 75¢ each additional book. (Colorado residents add 3% per copy sales tax).

☐ Payment enclosed ☐Please charge my: ☐ VISA ☐ MasterCard

Acct. #_____ Exp. Date_____

Signature_____

Name _____

Address _____

City _____ State _____ Zip _____

Mail to:

Alpine Publications, Inc., P.O. Box 7027, Loveland, CO 80537

REFERENCES

FURTHER READING FOR THE CURIOUS:

Bergman, Goran. *Why Does Your Dog do That?* New York: Howell, 1971.

Burnham, Patricia Gail. *Playtraining Your Dog.* New York: St. Martins Press, 1980.

Dunbar, Ian. *Dog Behavior: Why Dogs do What They Do.* Neptune, N.J.: T. F. H. Publications, 1979.

Fox, Michael W. *Understanding Your Dog.* New York: Coward, McCann and Geoghegan, 1972.

Haggerty, Arthur J. and Carol Lea Benjamin. *Dog Tricks: Teaching Your Dog to be Useful, Fun & Entertaining.* Garden City, N.Y.: Doubleday, 1978.

Lydecker, Beatrice. *What the Animals Tell Me.* New York: Harper & Row, 1977.

Mery, Fernand. *The Life, History and Magic of the Dog.* New York: Grosset & Dunlap, Madison Square Press, 1968.

Monks of New Skete. *How to be Your Dog's Best Friend.* Boston: Little Brown and Co., 1978.

Pearsall, Margaret E. *Pearsall Guide to Successful Dog Training.* New York: Howell, 1978.

Pfaffenberger, Clarence. *The New Knowledge of Dog Behavior.* New York: Howell, 1963.

Tortora, Daniel F. *Help: This Animal is Driving Me Crazy.* New York: Playboy Press, 1977.

Tortora, Daniel F. *The Right Dog for You.* New York: Simon and Schuster, 1980.

Whitney, Leon F. *Dog Psychology. The Basis of Dog Training.* New York: Howell, 1978.
Wolters, Richard A. *Family Dog.* New York: E. P. Dutton,

FURTHER READING FOR THE VERY CURIOUS:

Allen, Robert D. and William H. Westbrook, eds. *Handbook of Animal Welfare.* New York: Garland STPM Press, 1979.
Beck, A. M., "The Dog: American's Sacred Cow?" Nation's Cities 12(2):29-31, 34-35, 1974.
Burns, Marca. *Genetics of the Dog.* (Technical Communication No. 9 of the Commonwealth Bureau of Animal Breeding and Genetics, Edinburgh.) Commonwealth Agricultural Bureaux, Farnham Royal, Slough Bucks. 1952.
Campbell, William E. *Behavior Problems in Dogs.* Santa Barbara: American Veterinary Publications, 1975.
Fox, Michael W. *Canine Behavior.* Springfield: Charles C. Thomas, 1972.
Sauter, Frederic J. and John A. Glover. *Behavior, Development, and Training of the Dog.* New York: Arco Publishing Co., 1978.
Scott, John Paul and John L. Fuller. *Dog Behavior: The Genetic Basis.* Chicago: University of Chicago Press, 1965.
Smythe, R. H. *The Breeding and Rearing of Dogs.* New York: Arco, 1969.

BOOKS FOR THE INSATIABLY CURIOUS

Fox, Michael W. *Integrative Development of Brain and Behavior in the Dog.* Chicago: University of Chicago Press, 1971.
Hall, Roberta and Henry S. Sharp, eds. *Wolf and Man: Evolution in Parallel.* New York: Academic Press, 1978.
Pfaffenberger, Clarence et al. *Guide Dogs for the Blind; Their Selection, Training and Development.* New York: Elsevier, 1976.

INDEX